COUNSELLING CONVERSATIONS

10 POWERFUL INTERVIEWS WITH SEASONED EXPERTS

KIM BILLINGTON
M. Couns. M. Narrative Therapy. B.Ed

Illustrated by Chris Munro

First published by Ultimate World Publishing 2021
Copyright © 2021 Kim Billington

ISBN

Paperback: 978-1-922597-87-8
Ebook: 978-1-922597-88-5

Kim Billington has asserted her rights under the Copyright, Designs and Patents Act 1988 to be identified as the author of this work. The information in this book is based on the author's experiences and opinions. The publisher specifically disclaims responsibility for any adverse consequences which may result from use of the information contained herein. Permission to use information has been sought by the author. Any breaches will be rectified in further editions of the book.

All rights reserved. No part of this publication may be reproduced, stored in or introduced into a retrieval system, or transmitted in any form, or by any means (electronic, mechanical, photocopying, recording or otherwise) without the prior written permission of the author. Any person who does any unauthorised act in relation to this publication may be liable to criminal prosecution and civil claims for damages. Enquiries should be made through the publisher.

This book is educational in nature and does not constitute therapy advice. Please seek help from a professional if you require support.

Cover design: Ultimate World Publishing
Layout and typesetting: Ultimate World Publishing
Editor: Emily Riches
Illustrator: Chris Munro
Rear cover photo: www.susanbradfieldphotography.com

Ultimate World Publishing
Diamond Creek,
Victoria Australia 3089
www.writeabook.com.au

Testimonials

"*Counselling Conversations*, Kim Billington's new book, is like a community of practitioners that welcomes us, the readers, in. We are invited to participate, as witnesses, to conversations between Kim and the diverse group of counsellors and therapists that she interviews. Kim's own curious inquiries open up stories of people and practices that have roots in lived experience, in families, cultures and values, that are alive in their real worldness and deeply infused with wisdom. This book is a hopeful space, a meeting place, where it is possible to be part of the change we would like to see in the world."

Dr. Carla van Laar
MCAT DTAP AThR

"I enjoyed reading a wonderful conversation between two professional women in the interview with Jackie Tarabay, an experienced bereavement and trauma counsellor. It was an exchange of generous wisdom, stories reflecting on current loss and grief theories, practice and lessons learnt. Any counsellor will feel validated and encouraged by Jackie's story. What really touched me was Jackie's challenge with burnout and compassion fatigue – a common experience with dedicated counsellors."

Beate Steller,
Accredited Mental Health Social Worker, M.A.P.S.
M.A.Ed. B.S.W (Hon) R.N.

"Dajana's chapter about family violence helped me observe a practitioner's journey – from the moment you feel the calling, to the challenges, different paths, work and study undertaken to build knowledge and experience. This chapter is a roadmap for both beginner counsellors to envision their journey, and for practitioners more generally to have a resource with case reflections and pointers to bring to their own practice."

Niveen Rajabdeen
Mental Health Counsellor; Ayurvedic Lifestyle Consultant; M.Couns; BA / PGDip Psych; Dip Ayur; RYT, BCom, CIM (UK)

"Starting out as a newly qualified counsellor can be a daunting and somewhat unsettling experience. Rarely is there a wise master standing beside you to help guide you through this new therapeutic space – unless you're fortunate enough to be working alongside someone like Kim Billington. I first met Kim whilst working as a child counsellor for a not-for-profit organisation involved in family mediation and counselling, where Kim had worked for some years. We hit it off straight away.

I found Nothara's chapter about working in schools to be an insightful and honest account of how isolating working within a school setting can be for a practitioner. I am now a school counsellor in a wellbeing team. With over eight years in this role, I understand what a balancing act it can be around the expectations of the school, and your own responsibilities around your self-care. So wonderful to read a book compiled by a true artisan in the world of narrative therapy – about counsellors, for counsellors."

Penny Power
Child and Adolescent Counsellor; BA Coms; M. Couns

"*Counselling Conversations* brings together the experiences of ten different practitioners in their professional fields of counselling. Kim unites these stories with her own enthusiasm and vision, a passion for lives enriched and sustained through difficulties. In my position as supervisor, I have valued Kim's broad experience and academic background; they provide a firm foundation for her research and writing. I recommend this book as a valuable addition to the library of those in the counselling profession."

Dr. Vivienne Mountain
University of Divinity, CCAA PACFA AAOS

"I worked closely with Kim a number of years ago, co-facilitating groups for children who had experienced family violence. She sparked ideas for me in relation to thinking outside the box when working with children.

Her new book, *Counselling Conversations* is such a wonderful idea for those beginning their journey as a therapist, but also for those experienced counsellors who have been practising for many years. I enjoyed reading the interviews from such a diverse group of therapists. I will definitely be recommending this book to those counsellors I supervise and my colleagues."

Bronte Allen
Child and Adolescent Counsellor. Master of Mental Health Science, Graduate Diploma Child and Adolescent Psychotherapy, Graduate Diploma Music Therapy.

"The interviews were such a delight to read. Kim and I studied Narrative Therapy together at The Bouverie Centre in Brunswick 15 years ago. Reading about how Kim listens and reflects reminds me of how when I'm with Kim, talking about the challenges and joys in life, I feel I'm wrapped in a big, soft blanket that makes me feel safe and comforted. After I have talked in that safe cocoon she so naturally provides, the result is clarity, calm and comfort. The poetry section made me think of how cathartic my own song writing has been for my album, as a musician."

Josephine Dempsey
Nurse, Grad Cert. Narrative Therapy;
Grad Cert. General Nursing

"Kim has the courage to talk about the counsellor's inner world and the value of our own humanity as we navigate our own experiences. The book speaks to people really 'being with' people on their journeys. Tools/strategies/techniques have their place. However, Kim shows us the true value is in the relationship, the human connection, the desire to hold and cherish the strengths of another human being in the midst of their pain. I recommend this book wholeheartedly as an authentic way of walking alongside our clients."

Heather Goddard
Mental Health Social Worker

"There are ten insightful and engaging interviews with experienced mental health practitioners in Kim's new book, *Counselling Conversations*. Discussions of working from a reflective, trauma-informed and somatic-focused framework were particularly relatable to me as a trauma therapist.

Kim's well thought out questions and observations help unfold each practitioner's stories: how they chose their profession and how their personal experiences and choices inform their clinical work. These insightful and knowledgeable conversations would resonate with both beginner and experienced practitioners alike."

Linda Yan
Counsellor, B. Psych (Honours). M. Couns

"Kim's new book *Counselling Conversations* allows the reader to tap into the world of each counsellor, following their journey and getting a taste of what it is like to work in each specialised field. It is also a great starting point to explore the courses, counselling approaches, programs, and organisations in the relevant fields of practice explored in the book."

Stephanie Lai
Senior Counsellor and Creative Arts Therapist, BSW, BFA, MCAT

"*Counselling Conversations* was an enjoyable read, formatted as a conversational style between the author and therapy professionals. Therapists traverse a varied and interesting array of therapy approaches, client populations and personal reflections. The book also provides readers with a valuable opportunity for their own reflective practice whilst working in the field. The reflections are engaging and informative for anyone currently working in the psychological professions or wanting a deeper understanding of therapists' diverse and complex work."

Dr Sophie Lea
School of Educational Psychology and Counselling, Monash University. BTeach(Prim.), BEd, GCEdRes, MCouns. PhD.

"Even days after reading parts of the book, I would feel compelled to go back and read it again. I was drawn to the moments of clarity it brought to me. These moments have been invaluable to me as a therapist, enabling deep reflection into my practice with parents, children and caregivers. I can't wait to read more and delve into the distilled wisdom that is being so generously offered."

Bonita Mitting
Children's Counsellor/ Art Therapist. B.Arts, Grad.Dip. Ed., MTAP, AThR

Contents

Testimonials	iii
Acknowledgement	xi
Kim's Expression of Gratitude	xiii
Introduction: "Kim, you're writing a *second* book?"	3
Chapter 1: Wuru Walking in Two Worlds	13
Chapter 2: The Greatest Thing You'll Ever Learn…	27
Chapter 3: Family Violence Through the Lens of Trauma	47
Chapter 4: Outside My Comfort Zone	63
Chapter 5: Finding the Rainbow Connection	79
Chapter 6: Evolution Not Revolution: The Challenge of Simple, Hard Work	93
Chapter 7: It's Never Too Late…	107
Chapter 8: Releasing Hidden Creativity as an Aid to Therapy	123
Chapter 9: More Than Just a Counsellor	137
Chapter 10: Hearing the Voice of the Child: Working with Parents in the 21st Century	155
Chapter 11: Four Cornerstones of Counselling	171
Chapter 12: "You Can Land Safely Here," said the Blank Page	191
About the Illustrator	199
References by Chapter	201
Offers	211
Speaker Bio	213

Acknowledgement

Recognising Aboriginal and Torres Strait Islander people as traditional custodians of the land is one way to show respect for the indigenous peoples of Australia. Acknowledgement of Country says, "I see the connection of Aboriginal people and their history with land, place and culture."

I heard this powerful phrase from Professor and Director of Monash Indigenous Studies Centre, Lynette Russell AM:

"Every footfall is on Aboriginal land."

I take the opportunity in writing this book to speak with a voice that says, "I accept that sovereignty has never been ceded, and that this land was unjustly taken, and is illegitimately occupied."

Arriving in Australia as a 12-year-old in 1970, I did not understand the history of this beautiful country. It took decades to appreciate that whatever I was benefitting from was founded on the fact that my white ancestors and colonisers had knowingly acted with malice, broke all the basic precepts of humanity and that I was now basically in receipt of stolen goods.

I invite people to stand up, speak up and fire up about indigenous incarceration rates and other denigrating injustices and the abysmal lack of solution thinking by those with power. My hope is that more non-indigenous people will learn about colonisation and the impact on indigenous history and culture, through podcast interviews and autobiographies, and reflect about what each of us can do to Close the Gap and make restorative amends.

So today, I acknowledge the Elders and all those who identify as members and Traditional Custodians of the land of the Bunurung people of the Kulin Nation, past, present and emerging. I live, play and work on your land and I value your enduring connections to Country, knowledge, culture and stories.

Kim's Expression of Gratitude

I feel blessed to have met so many beautiful colleagues on my counselling journey. I particularly want to thank the wonderful collaborators who co-created this book.

Your swift embracing of the concept and assisting with editing and finding awesome quotes has been so affirming. The process required your hard work and prioritising chunks of time, and somehow, with a sprinkling of magic, this dream has come true.

I am grateful also to Dionne Hose, Hellena Bazán, Jenny Lo Ricco and Michelle Fairbrother who have generously contributed their lived-experience poems to this book. Your powerful heart songs are testimony to the rich and rewarding healing practice of poetry therapy.

My special thanks are to acclaimed artist, Chris Munro. I am uplifted by Chris's drawings, and his devotion to art. His fresh style and talents were complemented by his patience and enthusiasm through the draft sketches, and has made our work together a total delight.

Over many years, my clients have bravely picked up the phone, and subsequently arrived for that first session. Thank you from my heart's depths for your confidence in me. That was always a surprise. Your trust in me to receive and hold your sacred stories, struggles and hopes has enlightened me about the sanctity of counselling. I have cherished memories of so many turning points and sparkling news of change after dark times in your lives. You are the ones who did the hard yards of road-building your futures. You have taught me how to be the counsellor I am still becoming.

My gratitude reaches out to my supervisees who reconnect with me each month, to chew the cud of a wide range of often challenging experiences. I am honoured and warmed by your belief that I may be of help. Our conversations have brought me the bliss of professional satisfaction.

I also acknowledge and dedicate this book to the many senior counsellors who taught, shaped and inspired me as I learnt about this venerable vocation, in particular Ron Findlay, David Epston, Michael White, Irvin Yalom, Michelle Morris and Cheryl Taylor.

> "With mirth and laughter let old wrinkles come."
> — **WILLIAM SHAKESPEARE**

My energy, enthusiasm and passion for worldly ideas and finding a purposeful career was absorbed through my mother's milk. Wyn Billington was a warm, gentle and compassionate psychologist. Her last role was at Ishar, a women's multicultural health centre in Mirrabooka, Western Australia. Thank you to the women of Ishar, for appreciating my mum's gifts over those last 15 years, and for cherishing her, especially dearest Shobhana Chakrabarti. She adored you all.

"The essence of working with another person is to be present as a living being... So, when I sit down with someone, I take my troubles and feelings and I put them over here, on one side, close, because I might need them. I might want to go in there and see something.

And I take all the things that I have learnt – client-centred therapy, reflection, focusing, Gestalt, psychoanalytic concepts and everything else (I wish I had even more) – and I put them over here, on my other side, close... I just need to be present.

There are no qualifications for the kind of person I must be. What is wanted for the big therapy process, the big development process is a person who will be present.

And so, I have gradually become convinced that even I can be that. Even though I have my doubts when I am by myself, in some objective sense I know I am a person."

— EUGENE T. GENDLIN

INTRODUCTION

"Kim, you're writing a *second* book?"

This book grew from dream to reality through the generous sharing from my friends and colleagues who are professional counsellors and psychologists. Their many years of accumulated wisdom fill this book with exciting promise.

Each chapter has its treasures and practical examples of evidence-based interventions, modalities and approaches, with ample references to texts, favourite books and other resources listed by chapter at the end of the book.

Even whilst I was writing my first book, which became an Amazon #1 Bestseller, *A Counsellor's Companion: creative adventures for child counsellors, parents and teachers*, I knew there was more to share.

Tamar Dolev created dynamic and playful images for my first book, and I am delighted with local Melbourne artist, Chris Munro's fresh and engaging drawings in this second book, which were tailored collaboratively with the counsellors interviewed. My hope is that this practical and professional fireside book offers something for your soul, as well as your curiosity about how other practitioners have found and shaped their careers.

How This Book Took Shape

One day, I woke up with a sparkling new idea, picturing this very book. I even made a pencil sketch of the cover image. I could almost see the way the interviews would look, laid out across the pages. So, my next step was to make it happen. I reached out to my esteemed colleagues to find a way to gather and showcase their wisdom, and embarked on another creative adventure!

With an abundance of enthusiasm, I sent out invitations to be interviewed with a cherished hope that this would offer the reader a delicious banquet of practice wisdom around their work with adult clients.

I was so excited, but then panicked when The Imposter Syndrome came knocking on my door, especially in the weeks, hours and minutes before the first interview with Jackie Tarabay. Jackie and I shared our twin feelings of, "Who am I to do this?" and then we laughed together.

The Imposter still comes back from time to time, for an unexpected tango. I have learnt to acknowledge his presence, take a breath and get on with the job.

> "Our doubts are traitors,
> and make us lose the good we oft might win,
> by fearing to attempt."
> — WILLIAM SHAKESPEARE

Within these pages is a wealth of experiences. You will hear some beautiful stories and some painful ones: stories of the long roads my colleagues have travelled as they survived hardships, found their passion and forged their unique counselling careers.

Some of my interview questions have a narrative therapy style, and arise from my curiosity about how identity evolves and how people find meaning and purpose in their lives. How childhood experiences, or family values find their way into career choices. They are similar to the enquiries I find helpful in my client work.

I am inspired by Holocaust survivor, Viktor Frankl's life story, *Man's Search for Meaning*. Dr. Frankl said that "finding meaning and a sense of purpose" gave him the will to survive.

My Vision

From the beginning, I pictured you, the reader, sitting down in the evening or on the weekend with this book in your lap. I wanted to capture how it flows when counsellors catch up and chat about their wellbeing and their client work.

I wanted to offer you a sense that you are part of a broader group of professionals who have found and followed their passion. I wanted to offer you my encouragement to follow your bliss.

Whether you are a counselling student, an experienced professional, or someone looking for support, it is my hope that this book will answer many questions you didn't even know you had!

It has been a privilege to spend time with my fellow counsellors from so many different backgrounds, workplaces and client groups as this book was being created. These conversations which we recorded, transcribed and edited together have been uplifting, energising and inspiring for me.

Let Me Introduce You to The Team

The warmth, depth and richness of this book comes from a series of conversations in June 2021, all on Zoom!

Many interviewees shared afterwards that this process had been a healing opportunity, inviting them to pause and reflect how they have made sense of their choices, challenges and achievements in their careers.

Annette Dudley opens our book with her chapter "Wuru Walking in Two Worlds." Annette lives close to her Aboriginal and Torres Strait Islander culture, connecting her to Murray Island, Tanna Island and The Bailai Nation of the Gladstone area, in Central Queensland.

Wuru is Bylee language for black girl. Annette and I met whilst studying our Master of Narrative Therapy and Community Work at the University of Melbourne. Annette has so much to teach us about indigenous practice and narrative therapy, and has some important suggestions for understanding and improving working with indigenous families.

"The Greatest Thing You'll Ever Learn…" is a line from a special song with deep meaning for **Jackie Tarabay**. In Chapter 2, Jackie tells us her story of three personal, tragic losses, and the meaningful work she has found as a specialist bereavement counsellor at the Australian Centre for Grief and Bereavement. Jackie's philosophy towards grief and loss is that every person is unique and grieves in their own way and in their own time. Jackie believes the core qualities of genuineness, empathy and unconditional positive regard are at the heart of supporting the bereaved.

In Chapter 3, "Family Violence Through the Lens of Trauma," **Dajana Sprajcer-Simeunovic** shares her deep connection to the sciences, and demonstrates how she brings the research about the brain and body's role in responding to and healing trauma, directly into her clinical work with clients – all survivors of domestic abuse. Dajana discusses safety and so much more that you could not imagine unless you worked in the field. We could talk together about this topic for hours!

Susan Konstantas brings to Chapter 4 her journey of contribution which goes back generations, coming from a large family involved in caring roles in a small, close-knit town. In "Outside my Comfort Zone," Susan shares how she was drawn to counselling after 20 years in disability case management. With her love of learning and openness to new challenges, Susan shares what she has learnt working in many different counselling roles: family violence, palliative care and bereavement, hoarding, drug and alcohol and now in her own private practice.

In Chapter 5, "The Rainbow Connection," **Pamela Cox** speaks about her 45-year career as a psychologist and later as a supervisor, including her work in the rainbow community. Pamela's story offers key understandings about working with clients who identify as LGBTQIA+ and the long journey still ahead. I learnt so much interviewing Pamela for the book, and one standout was when Pamela said, "The process of coming out is never something that you do once; you do it your whole life."

Tom Lothian brings his fabulous blend of humour and professional spirit to Chapter 6, "Evolution Not Revolution: The Challenge of Simple, Hard Work." As a clinical psychologist specialising in the assessment and treatment of complex PTSD, Tom explains how he uses the trauma therapy phase model. Tom shows how he creates a safe space for a collaborative alliance, and progressive ways to support his long-term clients as they learn to self-regulate and tolerate emotional experiences.

I was so excited when Tom gave our artist, Chris Munro, a five stage suggestion for working with a client who has built a suit of armour in response to trauma. Chris immediately grasped the concept and metaphor, and eagerly created five incredible illustrations of a young person (with his skateboard) who is about to experience trauma. He perfectly translated Tom's methods into the visual, artistic realm.

In Chapter 7, **Robyn Ball** shares her wealth of experience working with parents using a well-known relationship roadmap tool called the Circle of Security. "It's Never Too Late… For Secure Relationships to Blossom and Grow" brings together key learnings from her attachment focused practice. Robyn guides parents to explore their responses to their child's distress signals, validate successes and repair ruptures in the parent-child relationship.

In Chapter 8, **Dalit Bar** takes us through the mysterious and reflective world of art therapy. In "Releasing Hidden Creativity as an Aid to Therapy," Dalit shares how her work began with her own love of art. Dalit finds art therapy offers clients a safe distance from big challenges, where unique insights, understandings and integration of identity can be expressed. Dalit shows how creative art activity with an art therapist can be a powerful vehicle to communicate life meanings, and heal after trauma.

In Chapter 9, **Nothara Suraweera** describes her exciting first counselling role in a regional secondary college. "More Than Just a Counsellor" follows Nothara's passion to listen and try to understand others. After the challenges of a migrant journey, and being the oldest of five siblings, Nothara transformed from being a "shy and reserved" teenager into a dynamic, courageous and professional welfare team leader in a high school. Nothara outlines her therapeutic practices and how she navigates the many challenges around ethical, boundary and confidentiality matters with students, parents and staff.

Chapter 10 is drawn from an interview by Natasa Denman, founder of author-mentoring service and publisher Ultimate 48 Hour Author. In "Hearing the Voice of the Child: Working with Parents in the 21st Century," Nat invites me to share some of my practical counselling approaches when working with parents. Topics include developing emotional awareness to break intergenerational patterns, re-parenting and staying connected with children through family meetings.

My initiation and stewardship of this book has allowed me to add some additional content:

Chapter 11, "Four Cornerstones of Counselling," is an offering of my responses to the FAQs from my Master of Counselling students over many years, such as: "What makes a good counsellor?" and "What *is* counselling?" It is a consolidation of what I see as foundational essentials for a beginner's practice, in particular one's relational stance and ethical requirements during that first session.

Chapter 12 holds space for some lived experience poetry: "'You Can Land Safely Here,' says The Blank Page." It introduces poetry therapy, which is close to my heart. Writing prose in my teenage years, and later episodic journaling, helped me understand and process many overwhelming emotions. As a counsellor, I was surprised and happy to discover that others also find relief from poetry writing as a form of creative expressive art therapy.

The Book Is Now Ready

This bold book lies in your hands, as a humble offering to those engaging in this so-called "helping profession." It is my belief that counselling is showing up, and "making ourselves available" for our clients, and colleagues. Whether this is "helpful" or not will be concluded, after due reflection and at some future time, by those who come to us seeking relief from their suffering.

May this book bring a sparkle to your day, warm your connection with yourself and other counsellors, as well as inspire future possibilities. May it be a catalyst for change. May our enthusiasm for the counselling profession brighten your journey and be a springboard for your creativity to flourish.

> "Seize the moment.
> Remember all those women on the 'Titanic'
> who waved off the dessert cart."
> — ERMA BOMBEK

REFLECTIONS

As you wander through the book, the following may be helpful guides on your own journey:

1. What attracts you to learning more about this field?

2. What might be a trigger for you with clients struggling with these problems?

3. Which phrases stood out as meaningful to you?

4. Imagine if you were asked to fill in for this counsellor for three months. What resources, people or mini-training courses might you seek to prepare for this role?

5. How transferable are your top three skills into this area of work?

6. What would you need to sustain longevity in this counsellor's role if the job was offered to you full-time? Or part-time?

7. What does this counsellor say about self-care that caught your attention?

8. Which book or resource caught your eye?

9. What might be one of your fears, and one of your joys, about going into this area of work?

10. What, for you, is at the heart of counselling?

11. What three challenges are you experiencing at this stage in your career?

12. If you look forward five years, where can you see yourself?

CHAPTER 1

Wuru Walking in Two Worlds

with Annette Dudley

Kim:
Since I've known you, you've been caring and being there for family members in the way I know that you'll be there for anyone. So where's that come from? When was it you first noticed that love from your heart, and that ability to be with people?

Annette:
Good question. I think coming from a big family, but also growing up I was really close to my nephews and niece, because we were around the same age. And I think going through life, we saw things in each other and people around us.

Kim:
So, when you say seeing things, you mean like people struggling around you?

Annette:
We didn't have a lot of money.

Kim:
Do you think that you were developing an understanding that other people had an inner struggle as well as an outer struggle too? You know, there's an outer struggle to get money or food on the table. When did you start to connect with this feeling that other people were struggling inside?

Annette:
I think that came from when I was younger, my mum and dad passed away when I was very young and later on I grew up in foster care. So, I had first experienced that internal struggle that you talk about at an early age. I lived with my big sister, and things weren't always great: we struggled financially and we went through some tough times. I suppose I didn't think about it until later on in life that we – myself, my niece and nephews – were going through a lot at the time, but as children, we didn't know any different. We just went to school and continued to be kids. After I had my first child, then I reflected on my own growing up.

Kim:
How was that when you were in primary school? Were you out there helping others, or were others tuning in to you?

Annette:
I think I was a bit of a loner. I only had a few close friends growing up and I wouldn't say that I was drawn to them so much. I think people were drawn to me. Some friends I grew up with, Suzanne, Vanessa, Tammy, Samantha, Raylene, Angela and Tony, all took me under their wings and noticed me. I didn't realise it but they probably saw me struggling, you know, at school and in different parts of my life. And they were there for me.

I fondly remember the Deputy Principal, Mr Bob Shearer who took me out of class and walked around the school with me when he saw that I wasn't having a good day. There were some teachers, too: Mr Mark Bolitho was the person who inspired my passion for writing. Mr Rodney Ballard and Mr Peter Griffin were people who I looked up to, they made a difference to my school days. These few people are some of the ones who contradicted the problem story in my life.

Kim:
Your way of honouring and paying tribute to others reminds me of your narrative letters in the Dulwich Centre documentary video, and another letter written to a problem that was in your life earlier using an externalised name: *Dear Streams of Stress*.

In our narrative therapy work, we often look for the history of the problem, and then the history of the alternative story. I'm thinking that you've had such tragedy as a little kid, but with your big sister, and your niece and nephews, who were at a similar age, you were kind of getting by. Then there were friends who saw you and teachers who inspired you, and that lovely story of the deputy principal making time in his day to help you sort things out.

Now you represent your community, and you've achieved the Master of Narrative Therapy, which is where we met.

Do people say, "Annette Dudley, she's a wise woman?" You're laughing!

Annette:
People come and talk with me, but culturally I'm not at that stage. I'm not an Elder.

Kim:
I don't think that "wise" was the right word. I'm thinking that people come along and see someone who feels stable, and strong enough to hear their story?

Annette:
I think it is a combination of many things. My life and work experience and knowledge, as well as my qualifications.

Throughout my younger years, I lived in a few foster homes and then there was one part of my life where I really struggled and I questioned everything around me. I questioned life, I questioned family. And, you know, I just felt really disconnected.

I suppose later on in life you think about these sorts of things, but, at an early age, we don't think about it. I completed Year 12, and then I decided I needed to get away and to do my own thing. So I left my home town, and I moved three and a half hours south to Rockhampton to go to CQUniversity.

Thinking about that inner struggle and that wisdom, I think that my life experience is where it comes from. It's not often I share my life story, but you know, when I think about people coming in and talking to me, and wanting to ask for information, or just to share my thoughts about something, I think that's where that comes from.

Kim:
And when people don't know your story, do you believe that they sense it anyway, spiritually, being in your presence? You know, I just imagined the metaphor of getting crushed, like coal under such pressure, part of you can become shining like a diamond, and that can be sensed by others?

Annette:
Sometimes when consumers get talking to me, they feel really calm, so that's a really good question. Yeah, I would probably have to ask them.

Kim:
I'm guessing you are feeling calmer after time with your Elders, too? You've shared with me that Elders have a strong presence and know things without having to say it. I'm sensing that culturally, part of your traditions, like Dadirri, already include these wisdoms and ways of being there for others. You show us this deep listening in your Dulwich Centre video. It is a very emotional experience to hear you read those letters.

Annette:
Do you know, it's that feeling that you get around Elders. It's just their presence that they bring. You can sense that when they walk into a room, you just know, by the way that they carry themselves and the words that they speak. You know there are little gems that you just want to grab and put in your suitcase and take away. The feeling you get is unexplainable, but one thing that comes to mind is that sitting with Elders and listening to them yarn is a privilege. A privilege to actually be hearing that story or that yarn.

And you know, it sort of gives me a warm feeling, like when you have that beautiful hot chocolate with your marshmallows in it. Where you feel filled with joy, and it gives you a big smile and inner peace as well. So that, yeah, when you're talking about that sort of stuff, that's what I think about. And that's how it builds.

Kim:
As soon as I hear you start talking about this wisdom that the Elders carry, I picture "sitting in the presence of spiritual energy" as I call it. I suddenly start to feel my heart almost shift or start to burn a bit, you know?

We talk about somatic therapy in healing, and listening to you today, I feel a powerful felt sense of my own heart expanding, even over Zoom! Do you feel a similar intensity? It's like on fire, really?

Annette:
Yeah, exactly, a feeling in every part of my body and it lifts me.

Kim:
I'm thinking a lot of people haven't got access to Elders, so they have to look for healing in other places.

We've got a friend in common, who's a psychologist we studied with. And he used to support the men out your way, and I had wanted to know if the men spoke to him about traditional stories that were healing for them, as I was studying storytelling and folktale therapy at the time.

I asked, "Do the men who you see share wisdom or healing through stories?" And he said, "I don't know. I'll ask them." And then he asked how the men's Elders convey their wisdom. And the men said to him, "Well, brother, you know, we are very grateful to you, but every week when we've said goodbye to you and the group's finished, we go straight to our Elders and they tell us stories!"

So, these men had access to their Elders, so maybe they had the best of both worlds, you know?

Annette:
Yeah, definitely, definitely. Another thing that really made that part of their healing journey special is that they were all on their traditional

Country. This strengthens that connection for them. It's such a beautiful way of living and walking in two worlds.

Kim:
You went to uni and studied different courses; can you share more about your career path?

Annette:
I was drawn to this area of working, and there was support and influence that enticed me to continue to go back and study. I think another thing that inspired me was the fact that I have a lot of family members who achieved university degrees.

Working in a community setting is important to me, and I'm seeing more young people completing Year 12 and furthering their education by enrolling in university.

Working with Elders and young people is where my passion is.

Kim:
I think we were fortunate to study narrative practice, because the skills and the techniques of narrative therapy feel in line with the traditional ways that you speak about.

I can't imagine how my counselling would be if I hadn't been on that journey. You know, people often say to me, "Kim, how do you think up these questions?" But it's literally the narrative approach that has been so helpful. It's centred on this way of being with a person who is struggling, in a way that doesn't impose anything, and where we explore parts of their life and values that invite rebuilding of personal agency, identity reconstruction, and repositioning to see new possibilities.

The questions often sound simple… but it's all very client-centred.

Annette:
It does sound simple, but sometimes it can be hard. Sitting down with someone and providing a safe space, and having a conversation in a respectful way as they get unpacking the problem story.

Kim:
Yeah, making space to hear these stories. And what comes to mind is a tangled ball of yarn, and that's the person's life and their problems, all these different threads everywhere. And then we can see one thread that's a bit different from the others. And we tease it out, we pull it out and say, "Oh, what's this? I heard you say this, tell me something more about that story. Why is that story important to you?" And then some sparkling new story of strength or hope is told, that contradicts the problem story. So, in narrative therapy, we're listening, wanting to hear these unique outcome stories. We want to be yarning, you know?

Annette:
Thinking about that ball, every time you unravel it a bit more, it looks different, the story looks different. You know looking at the multiple, layered threads in a different way can be so helpful.

Kim:
Love that new perspective of the ball looking different. You know, western psychology has come a long way. Fifty years ago, Carl Rogers broke the mould of Freud's earlier methods of analysis of a "patient" by professorial medical doctors. Rogers spoke about the benefits of the counsellor being "client-centred" and having "unconditional positive regard," empathy, and almost reverence for the client. People thought this was so radical, so controversial and not professional, because prior to that, the clinician was assumed to be the "expert" who had all the knowledge, could find out "what's wrong" with a person, and come up with answers!

Annette:
It's interesting when you're putting it in that way. That's what we do, show compassion and empathy when hearing about a person's lived

experience and the struggles that they've gone through. It shows how that genuine inquisitive relationship develops when you're giving them time and space to share what's happening for them.

We walk with our consumers on their journey, we look at their journey and engage with them to strengthen their foundations to allow healing.

Kim:
I'd like to ask about what is missing in our response to 'out of home care', too. So, Annette, you have a lived experience and understanding of foster care. There's a lot of indigenous children at the moment, disproportionately in care. Some might be in kinship care, which is better, but they're not with their families or near their Country. What insights would you give to counsellors or social workers working with the indigenous community so they have a better understanding of the things that might be helpful for these children?

Annette:
It's good that you asked that question, because I think one of the most common things that I've seen throughout my years of working in the community sector was that "tick the box" mentality; to say you have "done the cultural connection for young people" by recommending they attend NAIDOC events or other one-off activities.

Carers or staff in case meetings will think they can tick a box, and have met the cultural component/connection by taking a young person to NAIDOC week events. It's a lack of awareness that Aboriginal and Torres Strait Islander culture is a way of life, and involves a deep connection of body, mind, emotions, family and kinship, community, land, water and spirituality.

Non-indigenous workers in the field are often not shown the steps that it takes to actually gain that knowledge as well. Not everyone has the initiative or desire that drives someone to seek that knowledge. Workers may not be aware that they could ask questions, and they're not guided on where to go or who to ask.

I would like to think that this old "tick the box" way of practice is changing, that people are having different conversations and approaching the situation with more understanding to support our young indigenous communities.

What comes to mind when you asked that question, was that although the percentages are still not great, with a variety of support programs in place, which embed commitment to change and to Close the Gap, changes in the concept of cultural engagement can happen. Important healing cannot be fulfilled, and the wellbeing of each child in care cannot be met by attending one annual NAIDOC event. Culture and connection is a way of life.

Kim:
Yes, we need to find a better way to support these connections. Many non-indigenous people apply for and get a role in community, or in the cities. There's always a lot of positions going at Victorian Aboriginal Child Care Agency (VACCA) here in Melbourne, and in agencies in other states. Non-indigenous folk apply, they get a job, but they don't know what we've been talking about today. How might they begin? I have found reading actual history and autobiographies has been helpful for me, and attending indigenous cultural awareness training.

Can you suggest something else to make a difference and change the older ways of ticking boxes?

Annette:
Understanding a broad history of Aboriginal, Torres Strait Islands and South Sea Islands is important. One of the biggest misunderstandings is the diversity within each culture. In some situations, we do class ourselves as united, but the diversity of our individual cultural groups can be very complex. I've had many people say that they didn't know how to ask without offending anyone. There is often a genuine interest to learn.

Kim:
So, we need to get curious and ask? That sounds achievable. Before we finish today, I was wondering, unless you've got something else in particular, I was wondering what helps you get out of bed in the morning with your beautiful sparkle?

Annette:
Probably my five kids, Dylan, Matthius, Tori, Wade Jnr and Steph, and my fiancé Mustafa. There's my siblings Bronwyn, Cedric, Elaine, Kevin, Lee-ann, Lillian, Donna, Daniel and Naomi, my extended family and true friends. Knowing that I am blessed to wake up every day, do what I do, have what I have, and to not take anything for granted.

I think you have to have passion for what you do. I am so lucky that the people I am privileged to surround myself with and meet every day, inspire me to continue on my path at Wakai Waian Healing.

You know, sometimes I have mixed emotions and it is sometimes a struggle, but I think of significant people in my life, and I know that every day they struggle. They are facing bigger battles, but they push through and tell stories of their victories, and I am honoured to follow their lead.

I strive to offer multiple layers of my knowledge, hope and strength for others to succeed in finding their balance. You only realise how important this is after you notice the impact of losing that balance.

I think it will always be a work in progress for me. I go back to my Traditional Country as often as I can, and I'm guided by my Elders on a regular basis.

Kim:
I know you're a very humble kind of person, and I see how you are now living kind of in the middle: you look up to your Elders and you feel privileged, and then you are also a beacon, a light that inspires all these younger people coming through. And as you get older you will always

have this purpose and commitment with the younger community below you. And that's what I see anyway. I see how the people that work with you are so lucky to spend time with you, you know?

Annette:
Wow. It's interesting you say that because I'm privileged enough to be on a couple of local Boards: Darumbal Community Youth Service Inc. and Women's Health Information and Referral Service CQ Inc. I sit between, and have surrounded myself with the best of both worlds, a cohort of various generations.

Kim:
You're describing some strong and supportive connections. I often feel rejuvenated when I'm being with and giving to other people who seek out my acquired counselling skills, knowledge and support. It feels like maybe you have some of that happening for you too?

Annette:
I never consciously think of it that way. I give to them, but I think they don't realise what they give to me and contribute to my life.

Kim:
Like us, I think we've got that kind of friendship. Who knows why we're here in the world, and here we are as friends together. And it's always wonderful and heart-warming to have these conversations with you, Annette. Thank you so much.

Annette:
Thank you, Kim and you're welcome. You know I'm really honoured that you asked me, and I think it is such a privilege to be sitting down and having these types of conversations because, sometimes people don't get the opportunity to share these sparkling moments in their lives. This act of sincere, genuine curiosity is a special moment in time that will influence and shape my continued journey in life. Thank you so much.

Annette's Acknowledgement of Country and Bio:

I would like to acknowledge my Ancestors that connect me to Tanna Island, Murray Island and Bailai Nation of Gladstone. I extend this acknowledgement to the Elders past, present and future of the Traditional Custodians of the land that I live, work and play on and to the Elders who have taken me under their wing and have mentored, supervised and guided me, supporting me to do the work that I am honoured and privileged to do.

I was brought up in a small town in regional Queensland, land of the Yuwibara Nation. My childhood years were a time of very deep personal challenges due to unfortunate and unforeseen circumstances. My resilience grew stronger and my desire to help others in times of personal struggle shaped my career path and studies.

I received my Master of Narrative Therapy and Community Work from The University of Melbourne in 2015, and I am currently working at Wakai Waian Healing in Rockhampton, Queensland.

Crisis colours our perception of our past and our future. I've always wanted to be the person that not only listens to, but hears a person's life journey, the "sparkling moments" that contradict the "problem stories" and support the person to live their "preferred stories."

My career decisions have taken me in a full circle having worked in specific areas with Elders, the Stolen Generations, women, families and youth.

Email: dlzmmettswplsg@gmail.com

CHAPTER 2

The Greatest Thing You'll Ever Learn…
with Jackie Tarabay

Kim:
I was quite nervous before this very first interview for the book today, Jackie. The Imposter Syndrome is often just a few breaths away… So, how did you come to be in the role you're in at the moment and, in this field of work? Did it start when you were young?

Jackie:
Well, good question. I come from a family of five. I was considered 'the carer' and my family would always say, "here she goes again, she's brought home another stray friend." Mum was so accommodating. We had an open-door policy. You didn't have to call, you could just turn up. So, I think that wanting to help people has always been there for me. When I was 19, I created and facilitated a program to help women in prison at Boggo Road Jail in Queensland. I was interested

in reading books about people who'd had difficult times and wondered how they got through it? I was always curious about people.

Kim:
Right. So that curiosity was there back then?

Jackie:
Yes, I was curious when people had gone through major personal struggles and trauma. Trying to work out how some people fall in a heap and stay there, while others can fall in a heap but then pick themselves up.

I did ten years of voluntary work. I worked with Big Brothers Big Sisters, a youth mentoring program, and then developed and facilitated a program for young women at Parkville Detention Centre called "Don't Give it Away." The name literally was referring to not giving away your self-respect and what you believe in. I also co-created and started a youth program called "Reach for the Stars" with Jim Stynes. We worked together on that for three years and it's now evolved into a not-for profit organisation called Reach Youth, operating out of Collingwood.

Kim:
I'm wondering if there's people that are watching over you now, from your family or your early friendship groups? If they were sitting here today, and listening in, would they be nodding, "Oh yeah. That's Jackie." Is that what they would be saying?

Jackie:
Yes. They'd definitely be saying "that's Jackie," but the other thing they would also be saying is, "You have got to set boundaries for yourself!"

Kim:
Oh, wow!

Jackie:
Which I tend to really struggle with. Why "grief and loss" as a career? Well, death has been a constant companion of mine. My first significant loss was when I was 16. My father left the family unit and I never saw him again. Eleven years later I received a phone call and was told he had died. In my early 20s, my partner died suddenly and unexpectedly. However, the most profound loss was the death of my six-year-old son, Sam. It was his death that led me into the field of grief and loss.

Kim:
Such huge losses, Jackie. And I'm picturing these three men, you know, one by one having stepped away onto other journeys. Do you have a kind of a spirituality of what happens, or where people go when they die that help you make sense of your losses?

Jackie:
I do believe that there is something bigger than myself. I do believe I will see my son again one day, in one form or another. When Sam was dying, I knew I would be the one to tell him that he was going to die. But before I could do that, I needed to confront my own mortality. What does death mean? Where do we go when we die? I realised then, and I still believe this now, that it is about creating meaning that gives comfort. What gave both Sam and myself comfort was that we would see each other again in another world, another realm.

Kim:
Were you able to share that with Sam? Did he respond in a way that he could make sense of it at his age?

Jackie:
Yes, he did. He asked lots of questions. He asked, "What happens when you die mummy?" And I would use metaphors to try and help him make sense of it. I don't know where it came from Kim, but I remember this one particular day as clear as crystal.

Sam was diagnosed with a brain tumour at the age of five and subsequently endured nine months of chemotherapy and radiation. That created a lot of confusion for him.

On this day, he had woken up from a sleep quite tired and agitated. He was quite distressed and I knew that he wanted to talk about it, but we were both doing this dance. You know, he didn't want to upset me. I didn't want to upset him. And there was this moment where I spoke, it just came out of nowhere. I said, "Do you remember you came from another family before you came to this family?" And he said, "No, I don't." And I said, "Me neither, but when you leave this family, you go to another family."

I used the metaphor of a cocoon: "Your body is the cocoon. When you move into the next life, when you're ready to die, you fly free like a butterfly, and you'll have no cancer and you'll be kicking the footy." And he was so accepting of that. He could then ask more questions, and made the choice of wanting to be cremated versus buried, because he said, he wanted the ashes to be at home with us, you know. He was very clear on that. Yeah, so that's what happened.

Kim:
I can see that conversation about the butterfly opened up those other really important conversations. That's the power of the metaphor.

Jackie:
Yes, metaphors are helpful, absolutely. And also, because he couldn't do the things that he used to do, you know, because he was quite a fast and furious kid, and loved playing the footy and doing anything that was fast, that we had to try and find a new way of being for him. And it organically became drawings.

So, he was teaching us, and the artwork that he was producing was like, wow. And the last picture was a house, but there was a set of stairs that divided him and us. And he was in the attic of the house, and he was just laid on the bed with his little Rara, his security blanket.

That was his last picture. And he turned around and he said to my partner, "I'm ready to die. I can do this." Quite phenomenal, Kim. Yeah. So, I do believe that he's in this angelic world, and I do believe that one day I will meet him again.

> "And the day came when the risk to remain tight in a bud was more painful than the risk it took to blossom."
> — ANAÏS NIN

Kim:
Thank you so much for sharing such a personal story, Jackie. Because it's the storytelling that shapes meaning and connects us with the clients. We often go into different fields of work, whether it's family violence, or bereavement and grief like yourself, because we have some kind of connection or yearning to better understand what the heck it's all been about.

Jackie:
Exactly.

> "Life shrinks or expands in proportion to one's courage."
> — ANAÏS NIN

Kim:
And this was before you worked as a counsellor, really?

Jackie:
Yes, I always wanted to get into counselling or psychology. I dabbled and did a bit of psychotherapy and shamanic studies because I was quite interested in rituals and ceremonies. I studied neuro-linguistic programming and did a master's in that. I was always fascinated with the different ways that people express themselves.

It was after Sam died that I went to uni and did a Bachelor in Counselling. I did another year specialising in grief and loss, and then another year of trauma training. I feel like I've done this work all my life, but in terms of grief and bereavement, it's been for the last seven years.

Kim:
Because I've written a book about my work with children, people often say to me, "do you do anything other than child counselling?' Of course, I do work with many other client groups. Does that happen to you too?

Jackie:
Well, it's interesting because in my private practice, it's nice that not all my clients are grief and loss related. I have more adults than children too, which is lovely to have some diversity. But at The Australian Centre for Grief and Bereavement, obviously it's all death related.

Kim:
Yes, and that's how we met. I love that. You were there for me when I was struggling. I was working in a setting where all of the clients were family members of patients, and they were experiencing painful bereavements at a palliative care hospital.

On top of that, my own father was in his last months, on his journey out, and it was all too much. I soon realised I hadn't processed my own dear mother's death – a significant loss of this wonderful woman, ten years before. So, I was being crushed with countertransference with my clients at work. It all came together and I spoke with you, but mostly I recall I cried a lot in our single session.

My decision was to move out of bereavement counselling because I couldn't only see clients with that one presentation, one after another, every day. I had my own healing to do.

Jackie:
Yes. I can absolutely understand that. For me, I do tend to lean into the saddest stories, you know. When people come into counselling they are marinated in vulnerability. There is something quite sacred about that space.

Kim:
I don't think you can learn that necessarily at university.

Jackie:
Doing a degree gives you language, a language for things that I had been organically doing for years, such as actively listening, paraphrasing, empathic statements and so on. In addition, it gave me a framework, teaching me various modalities and approaches I could draw upon while working with clients. But the real learning came from my own personal experiences and from my clients. Learning to be with myself, to hold my own trembling self, my vulnerability first, then I could hold my clients.

Kim:
With the master's of counselling students I work with, many will generally say to me, "Oh, I'm studying counselling because I want to help people." I often reply with dramatic animation, "So, have we got this toolkit? Can we just tighten this here, and fix that there?" I say, "Look, we can be 'available' for the person that is right in front of us, and if this ends up being 'helpful,' then so be it." So, what we can do is listen and offer a safe space. We need to slow down and find out what the client is looking for.

Jackie:
Yes. I know what you mean, Kim, and I don't think a university degree really gives us that learning about how we hold the space. How we lean into it? You know? It can be quite terrifying for some people when they're bearing witness to clients in their complex grief, who could be pulling their hair out, screaming, and saying, "Why? Why did he kill himself?" I mean, that's not the time to say, "Let me just

pull out something from my toolkit and let's try this intervention." You know, the relationship is the therapy.

Kim:
And, as you beautifully said, we hold our own vulnerability and trembling in this work, and if you think you don't have countertransference in every session, you've missed it! Because we're two souls connecting, and we are bound to be moved by something in the session: this happens with empathy. A client's story may resonate with our own experiences and values. The issue arises when we lose some of our focus, energy and presence, and for a few fleeting moments we may be only half listening to the client, and more listening to our body inwardly crying. This can lead to projecting onto the client an image of how we coped, or how we think they should cope.

Jackie:
Oh, you said that so beautifully. That's exactly right. My body is my barometer, whenever I feel a charge within my body, I'm curious to know what is going on for me.

Kim:
Jackie, I'm guessing that when you were 19 or 20 and developing all these wonderful community programs, maybe life hadn't yet granted you the stillness you now have? I'm guessing you now have a more whole awareness? Does maturity give that to you? What do you think about that? Or did you already have that in your 20s?

Jackie:
No. I didn't have this stillness at an early age. I had somatic responses to certain events, but didn't quite have all the language for what I was experiencing. I began to embody the notion of stillness when I was forced to be physically immobile for a number of months. I had a radical hysterectomy at the age of 38. I sat with myself in deep solitude for many hours. And for the first time, I began the journey of having a relationship with myself. I began each morning with a daily meditation which consisted of listening to music in my garden,

purging. The evenings consisted of lighting candles, playing music while gently moving my body. I was asking myself those big existential questions, "Who am I? What is my purpose? How do I want to be in life?"

Answering these questions truthfully and with raw honesty resulted in me leaving my marriage. Wanting more, learning to accept that, and then having the courage to do something about it. It is one thing to recognise something, and another to have the courage to do something about it.

Kim:
That sounds like quite a journey of identity growth. I used that word "maturity" before, and your growth reminds me of an apple tree growing from a seed. As a metaphor, the trunk grows year by year, the branches and leaves are growing too. There might be no fruit the first year, but when the tree is ready, the flowers drop off and the fruits begin to grow in their place. You know? And I feel that I'm speaking to you as a mature human being, where you've gone through significant growth and accomplishments, as well as losses, on the journey to coming to know who you are. And you talked about this connection to yourself...

Jackie:
Yes. The journey to connect with myself was painful, and yet liberating and powerful. I got to know me, the good, the bad and the ugly… I began the process of learning to love and embrace all sides of me. This continues to be a work in progress! What was most powerful was the process itself, meeting my biggest fears, allowing them to engulf me, consume me. I would go into my well and meet the agony. Each time emerging in a foetal position, sobbing and hearing myself whisper, "and I am still here." When Sam was dying and I could feel the hopelessness and the helplessness suffocating me, I would go into my well, meet the agony… "and I am still here."

Kim:
So, this connection to self has become important when working with clients too, Jackie. Do you become aware of your own vibrational resonance to the content of the client's story, as they're going through some emotional upheavals or regret, blaming, anger and bargaining, and all those different things that emerge with grief? So, from that

place of stillness, you "lean in?" I'm wondering if in that leaning in, your eyes can see their tears and the sobbing, and your body can sense what they are going through? Your body becomes a sense organ, sensing their body's emotional expression.

Jackie:
Yes. It's like your body knows something, doesn't it?

Kim:
Yes, and it's not something that I was capable of using when I started out, but now I'm becoming acutely aware of and doing so much more somatic work. Even with phone counselling, I say to people, "Can you put the phone on loudspeaker and put your hands on the heart, and the belly, and let's take a breath in. And as you let it out, press a little bit. What's happening? What's your body saying to you?"

Jackie:
Beautiful.

Kim:
I'm wondering how you work with your clients, too? If sometimes your clients ask you to give them homework? What do you offer when people want structure? Do you set goals?

Jackie:
Well, it's interesting. It absolutely varies, Kim. And you know I really believe if we truly listen to our clients, they teach us what type of therapist we need to be. I've had clients who've come in with a notebook and go, "Right. I want some strategies and I need homework." And I go, "Alright, thank you for telling me that."

If someone comes in with an enormous amount of guilt, I may say, "I want you to write a letter to your guilt. I want you to free associate. I don't want you to look at the grammar. I just want you to write a letter to the guilt." Another great intervention is inviting our clients to write a letter to the deceased, and then respond as if it was the deceased writing back.

Kim:
A bit like the empty chair? Making space for unspoken words?

Jackie:
Yes, like the empty chair. I also have many clients who are experiencing an existential crisis, a lack of connection and meaning in their life. This makes a lot of sense to me because often when we have suffered a significant loss, our assumptive world is shattered. Our assumptions or beliefs create a sense of predictability and safety in the world, and when this is destroyed, we can become unhinged.

Kim:
I'm wondering if you have sometimes found the creative expressive arts helpful?

Jackie:
Yes, I use several creative techniques to help clients share their stories. They consist of play therapy, sand tray, music, painting, clay, movement and creative work such as collages, grief masks, making calm down jars, just to name a few.

Kim:
What about mindfulness and grounding with grief work? Can you share a short practice or intervention when someone is quite distressed?

Jackie:
I like to use the dual awareness, flashback protocol and basic grounding techniques. All these are done in-session first, so clients have an understanding of how to use these outside of the counselling room.

Kim:
That's so interesting, I haven't heard of that. I'll look that up, and we can share a link in the references. And do you have a favourite inspirational quote, or poems you share with clients?

Jackie:
Viktor Frankl comes to mind:

> "The last of the human conditions is to choose one's attitude."

When shit happens, and it does, this is what we have control of, the attitude we choose. I also love Kahlil Gibran's work. He has written beautiful poems on love, death, marriage and children.

> "Your children are not your children.
> They are the sons and daughters of Life's longing for itself.
> They come through you but not from you.
> And though they are with you, yet they belong not to you."
> — KAHLIL GIBRAN

Kim:
I was also introduced to Gibran's work in 1985, through that same poem, "On Children." It was written and laminated on a lift in the Royal Women's Hospital in Melbourne, in the Jesse McPherson Wing. When I gave birth to my first child Claire, she was in an incubator and I could only go down and look at her. She was all naked under these cold, ultraviolet lights. I wasn't even allowed to touch her in those days. So, three or four times a day, I'd be reading that lovely poem through a hundred tears as I shuffled into the lift, to see her in that little plastic crib in the basement. And that poem is what got me through.

Jackie:
Well, that's the poem I read at Sam's funeral. Yeah. I think it's quite a powerful poem.

Kim:
Poems and quotes can crystallise and make wisdom accessible. I'll be making a safe place for some poems in the final chapter of this book.

We often come to points in our lives when we have to make some meaning, so that our experience makes sense. Counselling can offer that safe place for all that processing.

Jackie:
Yes, we are meaning-making machines.

Kim:
And as you've pointed out, when we experience a significant loss, all these assumptions about expectations of life and how life should be are no longer valid, and we have to shift towards a new set of beliefs to begin again.

Jackie:
Absolutely, it's like a rebuilding of self.

Kim:
And I've got a big question for you. What are your biggest fears in this work?

Jackie:
My biggest fear is reaching a point of complete burnout and compassion fatigue. I often struggle to set clear, healthy boundaries for myself, and I fear this may one day result in me walking away from this work for good.

Kim:
So how many times have you almost reached burnout in your career?

Jackie:
I would say at the end of last year. And I actually think I'm still in the midst of it.

Kim:
What are the symptoms for you, Jackie?

Jackie:
Physical and mental exhaustion resulting in a lack of empathy, low tolerance and disengaging from family and friends.

Kim:
Oh, was that why we didn't go on those lockdown walks?

Jackie:
Ah, I know Kim, I even had seven weeks' holiday, but I was still exhausted. I thought, "This is crazy."

Kim:
We don't necessarily go shouting from the rooftops about our close encounters with burnout. We more often hide it, and cut off conversations about what's really happening.

Jackie:
No, we don't often talk about it, but we should.

Kim:
There's a lot out there at the moment about self-care. We have been subject to some challenging pandemic lockdowns. I read Rick Morton's book, *My Year of Living Vulnerably*, and he used this phrase when talking about self-care and self-kindness: "radical compassion." That's what we need. He wasn't the originator of the term by any means, but it arrived just when I needed to hear it.

Jackie:
I'm going to look that up. That's what I need too.

Kim:
And I think humour can fall away too – the disappearance of humour?

Jackie:
Yes, yes!

Kim:
So, when you've not been as deep in burnout as you are now, and you catch it a bit earlier, what have you done to turn the corner in the past?

Jackie:
I have reintroduced my gratitude journal to shift my viewpoint, because when I'm tired and exhausted, the lens through which I view my world is more pessimistic. Every morning I try and go for a walk, and take the time to look up and notice three things that I feel, see and hear. All attempts to keep me in the present moment.

Kim:
So, being in nature?

Jackie:
Nature is a big thing for me: it's grounding.

Kim:
As often happens with patterns we have, there's a connection, a thread to someone else in our lives, often in our family of origin, who may love nature, for example, or have difficulties with boundaries! When you look back at your aunties or grandparents, who else also had this passion to help, and they also might have kept pushing themselves, and kept giving?

Jackie:
It was, and still is, all the women in my family. My mum, my aunties and everyone in our family of origin think that to actually sit down and have a cup of tea was considered lazy. My partner has been great for me. If I say, "Oh my God, I've done nothing all day." He'll say, "Jackie, you have done everything. You have filled your cup."

"To keep a lamp burning we have to keep putting oil in it."
— MOTHER TERESA OF CALCUTTA

Kim:
How beautiful. This gets me thinking how earlier in the 20th century, everyone had a day at home on a Sunday, or a Saturday in some communities. We've lost that day somewhere. Maybe we lost our recovery time? My mum, who was a psychologist, never worked on a Wednesday. She guarded that as her sacred day. She used to say, "That's my Christmas Day," and she would lie around in the sun, swim, read or listen to the radio and sew. She worked part-time with her clients until a week before she died, age 77, from a sudden stroke. She never booked a client on a Wednesday. What a smart woman.

Jackie:
What a smart woman. Yeah. I used to take myself on a date once a week. I need to reintroduce that back into my life. I loved it!

Kim:
When you've hit rock bottom, you don't realise it until you've crossed that final step. It's too late for a warm bath then. A bath ain't going to help you when you hit rock bottom. There's even a poem I wrote called "Rock Bottom Friday" in the last chapter.

Jackie:
You're a hundred percent right, Kim, it's really about catching yourself before you hit rock bottom.

Kim:
I'm wondering is there a significant learning that you haven't shared already, or a pearl of wisdom? If someone was saying, I think I might be interested in going into bereavement counselling, for example, is there a certain way they need to be, or should they have a particular strength? Is there anything obvious?

Jackie:
I would encourage people to understand and discover what the power of presence can do in-session. Learn to bring your whole self into the room. It's about forming a deep human connection.

"You cannot save people, you can only love them."
— ANAÏS NIN

Kim:
I can find myself depleted after a full day of clients, or on an adrenaline rush! I might be running low on the capacity to be present. I am good at keeping to 50-minute sessions, but also, I can find it hard to say no to squeezing in one extra "urgent" appointment. I can end up thinking, "Look, Kim, just get through this, and then you can let go." Which is not ideal.

Jackie:
I know Kim, I've noticed that too. I've had to create some hacks for myself to be fully present. One of them is to light a candle five minutes before each session; this helps bring me back into the present moment.

Kim:
What a beautiful image of finding ways to come to stillness to prepare ourselves to receive the client and their sacred story. Thank you so

much for today, Jackie, and for sharing your precious stories, and how you have been learning about yourself and the counselling role along the way. Any ideas for a title for your chapter?

Jackie:
Thank you, Kim. Yes, I'm thinking, "The greatest thing you'll ever learn," as the great David Bowie sang "…is just to love and be loved in return."

Bio:

Jackie Tarabay is a specialist bereavement counsellor, clinical supervisor, trainer and facilitator of support groups at the Australian Centre for Grief and Bereavement (ACGB). Jackie provides individual counselling to children, adolescents and adults, and also facilitates workshops, programmes and customised trainings. In addition, Jackie has presented at a host of national and corporate conferences as well as being part of expert focus groups. Jackie also runs her own private practice.

Email: Jackie Tarabay Counselling, jackietarabay@gmail.com

Qualifications:
Bachelor of Counselling (BCouns); Grad Cert in Bereavement Counselling and Interventions, Certified Bereavement Practitioner (CBP); Cert IVTAE; Diploma of Shamanic Studies; Master in Neuro-Linguistic Programming (NLP).

CHAPTER 3

Family Violence Through the Lens of Trauma

By Dajana Sprajcer-Simeunovic

Kim:
Thank you for agreeing to be interviewed for the new book, Dajana. I've known you for a few years, but I really don't know how you pictured yourself moving towards this career from when you were a little girl. What did you think you might be when you were little?

Dajana:
Thank you for your invitation, Kim. When I was little, I thought that I would be a doctor. While I was growing up, I was interested in listening to other people's stories, and different family members (including my two brothers) would come and tell me all about their problems.

In my late teens I had an interesting discovery about myself being able to listen, provide support and keep the stories confidential. I then studied to be a medical doctor and practiced medicine for several years.

Kim:
And you have a migration story, which is a story that both disrupts and offers something new?

Dajana:
It has been a powerful experience that has shaped me in many ways. I began to be much more oriented towards my inner world and developed an interest in psychological health. In Australia, I started volunteering for Lifeline and that's how I discovered counselling. Having a medical background was relevant as I always thought the connection between the mind and body was important. It felt like I finally found myself.

Kim:
Well, it sounds like you went looking for yourself, so of course you'd find yourself!

Dajana:
Exactly, because the first career was more about my family. My father was a doctor, and my grandfather was a doctor.

Kim:
So quite a family tradition! Then you came to Australia, and started working at Lifeline. Did you have your own family by then?

Dajana:
Yes, I had my two children and my husband, and I was discovering a whole new world in Australia. Lifeline helped me feel connected to people from various cultural backgrounds.

Kim:
Yes, and hearing all those stories on a 24/7 crisis line? How did you manage that? I've also worked for three years at On The Line, with

really difficult phone calls on MensLine and their other crisis lines. It was quite full on. There were people calling in who were really struggling, and often without supports around them. So, how did you personally manage that?

Dajana:
We all carry our own vulnerability and life story with us. I believe it was the right time for me to be there as it resonated with me. I felt privileged to hear their stories and to be there to provide a safe space.

Kim:
Safe space: this is such a huge thing. And, for people reading this chapter who might be thinking, "Oh, I'm not going to go down the family violence counselling path," how did you make the transition from phone counselling to family violence?

Dajana:
After two years at Lifeline, I decided to study my Graduate Diploma in Counselling and got a counselling job at a different helpline.

I am so grateful for that Lifeline experience. When I look back at my life, I see it as a life-changing time for me.

Soon after that, I decided to pursue further studies and enrolled into the Master of Counselling course at Monash, where I met you as my clinical supervisor.

Kim:
And your university placement was in family violence.

Dajana:
I'd had some previous experience in family violence through Victims of Crime services, but the placement was in a particular, highly specialised agency. I learnt that although family violence is clearly defined, I should not make any assumptions, as each person's experience is unique.

Kim:
So true, and much of the lens about this work includes trauma.

Dajana:
That is why I decided to expand my knowledge in complex trauma-informed counselling.

Since I started working as a qualified family violence counsellor, I've been working with children and adults and benefited so much from having you as a supervisor. The Master of Counselling course provided a great foundation, however due to the complexity of family violence counselling, I've also done quite a few courses post graduation.

Three seminal works by van der Kolk, Rothschild and Fisher are my favourite books, as well as courses on complex trauma through The Blue Knot Foundation. I found Janina Fisher's work the most inspiring and have done several courses with her. Sensorimotor psychotherapy including Pat Ogden's and Bonnie Goldstein's work shed a light on the role of the body and implicit memory in therapy. I've also done trainings in Acceptance and Commitment Therapy (ACT) and Internal Family Systems (IFS), and found the Australian Childhood Foundation Conferences (ACF) helpful too.

Kim:
Really that reminds me how you were transitioning from being a doctor into counselling, and you said that you had this understanding or this sense for the mind and body connection. This is the beauty of being a practitioner in the 21st century, because we now know that the body doesn't just keep the score, the body has all these stories to tell, and the body awakens us with its energies to pay attention to it. It is such a wonderful time to have these understandings.

Dajana:
Yes, absolutely. And with my scientific mind, I'm so into neuroscience and its contributions to understanding the stress response and hypervigilance that clients often present with. Introducing

psychoeducation and the role of the body in calming the amygdala, as well as mindfulness has been so helpful. One of the most important things I learnt was the phased approach to complex trauma and how important safety and stabilisation is, which is especially important with family violence.

Of course, we also talk about the woman's physical safety and how important it is to assess the safety of the children.

Kim:
Although we are speaking here about women, we acknowledge this problem is present in all relationships, including people from the LGBTQIA+ community. We know that men also suffer abuse and coercive control in relationships. Still, there is a disproportionate impact on women and children, who suffer from many power imbalances socially and culturally, as well as the ongoing terror of the threat and real possibility of lethal force.

We can never guarantee safety when a client is reporting about family violence. We can do a few things that might increase safety, like risk assessments and safety plans, installing CCTV cameras, organising AVOs and finding funding sources for relocating, but a lot of new counsellors still studying may somehow think that if the client calls the police, then everything will be safe. It's quite a myth, isn't it?

Dajana:
It is important that police are called as they have special powers to intervene, and put in place immediate protections like a Family Violence Safety Order. In Victoria, that means that the perpetrator of family violence is removed, and no contact is allowed.

Kim:
I say to new students coming through that you can guide the person towards increasing their safety, but as often happens, they may turn around and say, "well, no, I won't be going to court and getting an intervention order, or going to the police because last time I did

that, it made things worse." And really, we must believe the client because they know exactly who this perpetrator is, and what harm that perpetrator is capable of. We have to take our mandatory steps, but we don't have much control over outcomes.

Dajana:
Yes, and I believe that my role as a family violence counsellor is to support the client, provide safety information and help them explore the options. I have worked with women who were still in a relationship, and counselling helped them decide whether to separate or apply for an intervention order. As practitioners we also have a duty of care, to make a mandatory report, or call police for welfare checks. This is always discussed in the first session around confidentiality, and child safety in particular.

Kim:
And when one parent has been subject to intimate partner violence, the children are affected because they are in the same house. Their sense of safety gets lost. They are under duress, but it's all out of their hands.

I often found it disappointing that a phone call to Child First, or Orange Door (access points to Child Protection and support services in Victoria) to make a notification could become just a paper trail if the case wasn't forwarded to Child Protection for investigation, because it was not deemed of sufficient risk.

Dajana:
Yes, and a phone call directly to Child Protection around an imminent or high-risk case is always investigated at their intake level. If police attend the family violence incident with the children present, they provide L 17 referrals to family violence services and Child Protection.

I have had to work closely with police and Child Protection. Care team meetings are important in providing collaborative approaches in supporting the families.

I have found psychoeducation on the impact of trauma on the children and their behaviours also contributes to a better understanding of family violence dynamics to the women I work with.

Kim:
Many of the women are survivors/victims not just from this relationship, but from their own childhood traumas. I can't recall a single case in all my years of a woman saying, "I came from a completely safe, respectful home. No, as a child, there was no alcohol, no drugs, no violence, no frightening power dynamics no, nothing."

I don't think I can remember a case ever like that.

Dajana:
It has been my experience as well. The presence of intergenerational trauma is common, and the role of the parents' primary attachment is significant in the upbringing of children. I often quote from Dr. Daniel Siegel and Mary Hartzell's book, *Parenting from the Inside Out*:

> "It isn't what happened to you in your childhood that is the critical factor, it is how you make sense of how these experiences have influenced your life."

Kim:
Which is why the psychodynamic approach you've been studying has been especially helpful when doing this psych ed with these survivor/victims.

Dajana:
Yes, as you know, I recently started my second Master in Mental Health – Psychodynamic Psychotherapy. I am finding it helpful in contextualising the early attachment patterns and translation of the relationship templates into adulthood. I am hoping that it may assist parents relate to their children in a different way.

Kim:
Tell me if I'm wrong, but a lot of the women that we work with who have lived in constant shame and fear can enter a "freeze" response, which is the brain's choice of a safe, survival reaction. How that can then sometimes block their awareness of the impact the abuse is having on their children. Even after separation, there can be stalking and cyber abuse. The women have been living in such terror and are in survival mode, so they maybe can't really sit back and reflect on what this is like for the children.

Dajana:
Absolutely, because trauma is about disconnection from the self and others. Clients often say that one of their therapy goals is to be better able to understand their children and connect with them. This reminds me of another quote from Dr. Frank Anderson's book, *Transcending Trauma:*

> "Trauma blocks love and connection
> and healing our wounds provides access to the love and
> goodness that is inherent in us all."

Kim:
That is so true. And people new to family violence work may not realise that if the child is sitting in their own bedroom, they may not be "witnessing" things, but can be filled with terror from repeated cycles of violence. Children may try and fix the broken door, or help mum get an ice pack later on, or pick up the pieces of mum's mobile phone that's been smashed. It's the effects of these things around them that create awful, cumulative harm. In what should be their little safe home, fear becomes the normal response to these adult behaviours. Living with such high levels of stress and hypervigilance, their brains often choose a freeze response, as it's unsafe to enact fight or flight.

Dajana:
It is very disturbing for children to witness family violence directly, as well as to hide in fear alone or with siblings. For children to be present in the aftermath of the incident is so impactful that it now constitutes a family violence crime.

Kim:
Children are often doing their best to stay loyal to both parents, too, and as they will probably have supervised contact with the abusive parent. They can be conflicted, and don't want to be seen as taking sides, so the stress never quite goes away.

Dajana:
Yes, and it can be retraumatising for the children to have those supervised visits.

Kim:
It can be a deeply disturbing area to work in, where every day we see such innocent, vulnerable children harmed by the very people they are born to trust.

Your therapeutic work has had many successes. It might be good to hear some examples of how you implement the phased treatment approach to complex trauma around stability and safety.

Dajana:
Stephen Porges, the founder of the Polyvagal theory talks about the concept of *neuroception*: the body's feeling of safety that is unconscious and precedes the conscious perception of safety. Porges noted that safety does not mean just the absence of danger, but the presence of connection with another person. Creating safety is the most important part of my work with both adults and children.

> "If you want to improve the world, start by making people feel safe."
> — STEPHEN PORGES

Kim:
What kind of things do you do when you're with children and women for those first few sessions?

Dajana:
It's important to give the children a choice to be in the session with their secure parent initially. That has been helpful in decreasing anxiety about therapy in both the parents and the children. Explaining what counselling is and being transparent is essential in creating safety. Safety refers to physical, emotional and relational aspects. Children usually like to come to the office as there are many resources for them. Informed by child-centred play therapy, I let them choose what to do. Sometimes, in the beginning, they may want to leave the session early, especially the younger children, and that's ok.

Kim:
This reminds me of how in a classroom setting, a teacher expects a child who's come from a home where there's been family violence to sit still for 40 minutes, and stay at school all day when they may well be experiencing stress fatigue, and possibly preoccupied with worry about mum's safety.

Dajana:
Yes, and we know that movement is an important tool in emotional regulation.

Kim:
I've been enjoying using Dr. Robert Grant's interventions. He works with children on the spectrum, and his AutPlay activities are mostly involving movement, which is ideal for trauma therapy.

But let's talk a little bit about working with the adults.

Dajana:
I believe that therapy needs to be individualised and I combine different modalities and tools depending on the client's need and presentation. I use trauma-informed and strength- based approaches and usually introduce grounding skills and work with exteroceptors early in therapy. Sometimes clients present in a crisis, and according to Maslow's hierarchy of needs, careful assessment and pacing is imperative.

Kim:
And tuning into how their body is speaking as well? We really need to help our clients gradually reconnect with their body when it is safe to remedy dissociation.

Dajana:
I use one hand on the heart and the other one on the forehead, and then one on the belly – it's one of my favourite somatic resources. It's important that we make no assumptions and stay curious. Noticing five things they can see, hear and feel. Feeling their feet on the floor and pushing them is the grounding exercise many people find helpful. It's supporting them moving from exteroception into interoception, when they are ready. I use it often myself in my own self-care.

Breathing is an excellent resource and I always give clients the option to try it. Still, some clients who have experienced trauma may be triggered by breathing exercises. So, a deep sigh can be introduced instead, as it has a long exhalation and is followed spontaneously by deep inhalation. Progressive muscle relaxation and simple strategies like movement, rocking, going for a walk, splashing cold water over the face, slowly drinking cold water or changing the posture can be helpful too.

Kim:
So moving from outer, external awareness to inner sensing, and exploring tailored breathwork, it's like we can offer a menu of interventions, and each client will tell you what works for them.

Dajana:
I like to ask that question in the early sessions. How did you cope in the past? What helps when you feel stressed out? Helping clients

access their inner resources and bringing their awareness to it is crucial. Sometimes calling a friend and co-regulation by a trusted other is all they need to help them regulate.

Kim:
Dajana, have you been thinking to yourself, "I might try something different with this new Masters in Mental Health?" Have you thought, "I wonder what I might do next?"

Dajana:
I've been thinking of starting my private practice, and have already begun some preparations.

Kim:
Oh, that's so encouraging to hear. That's wonderful. And what about moving into the role of a supervisor? Because you've gathered such a wealth of experience now. Is that something that you'd like to do as well? I would love to see you do that.

Dajana:
Maybe, I haven't thought too much about it.

Kim:
I have found that transition of giving back to our profession quite rewarding, though I still work as a counsellor too.

We learn so much from our clients who have endured harrowing stories, and yet have somehow held onto hope. They show us something which can help us keep going in this field.

Dajana:
There is wisdom within each person. The passion for this work is what keeps me going. I feel energised after sessions, and that's how I know I am ok. If I start feeling a bit tired or notice that I'm not keeping my boundaries clear, I know that I need to do my self-care better.

Kim:
And what kind of things are part of your self-care?

Dajana:
I often do micro self-care in session if I notice changes in my breathing or my posture. Simple things like changing my position, lowering my voice, slowing my speech and feeling my feet on the ground can be helpful. I always stretch and move between the sessions, or apply light hand pressure on my arms, and use aromatherapy. I keep my hand cream and soap handy so I can smell them between my sessions.

> "Nothing can cure the soul but senses."
> — OSCAR WILDE

Kim:
Yes, these soothing smells, they go straight to the brain.

As soon as you said aromatherapy, I pictured the little molecules of compounds taken in through the nose, and the brain saying, "Oh, thank you!"

Dajana, talking about these aromas is just what I needed after this heavy topic. I'm better regulated already, just imagining the smells. Now the window of tolerance is nice and wide.

Dajana:
Yes, exactly! And there is the risk of vicarious trauma when working with such intense cases, especially where children are involved, so we need to practice our self-care.

Kim:
And if we can get our self-care right, the work can be so rewarding. Thanks so much for coming today.

Bio:

Dajana Sprajcer-Simeunovic has worked with clients for over 15 years in the fields of family violence, addiction, crisis telephone counselling and supporting victims of crime.

She is currently studying towards a Master of Mental Health - Psychodynamic Psychotherapy. Dajana specialises in family violence and complex trauma counselling with children, individuals and families impacted by family violence.

Dajana has two adult children and loves spending time in nature with family and her dog, Lola. In her free time, Dajana enjoys folk dancing and poetry.

Email: sdajana@yahoo.com

Qualifications:
Family Violence Counsellor; M. Couns; GradDip Couns; Dip AppSci

CHAPTER 4

Outside My Comfort Zone

with Susan Konstantas

Kim:
Hi Susan, great to have you here. You've had a broad range of experience from two decades as a disability support case manager, to seven years in various counselling roles. Where would you like to start?

Susan:
I've learnt we don't know who's going to come through the door on any given day. We have to find our way and tap into new ideas, and find people who can support us with growing our skills and knowledge. When I was new to counselling, that was one of my biggest fears, my knowledge gap.

With time and experience, I've found I don't need to know everything or to be everything to all people! I now focus on the first session to build rapport with my clients and make that my main priority. As a person-centred counsellor, I believe that my most important job is to connect with my clients and for them to feel heard. So, at the end of that first session, they can walk out the door thinking, "I felt understood and listened to… I felt supported and safe to talk about whatever issues I brought to the space."

Kim:
That safe, therapeutic connection is so central to counselling. What is step two in your practice?

Susan:
I need to find out what the client wants from counselling, and how we might best work on their issues together. I can now accept that this might take a while. Taking time and not rushing is essential from where I sit, and knowing that everyone who comes to counselling is different, they're all unique.

Even though I've being qualified as a counsellor for seven years, I continue to think of myself as a 'new' counsellor because I feel like I have so much to learn and there's so much I want to learn. My growth mindset keeps me on my toes.

> "The expert at anything was once a beginner."
> — HELEN HAYES

Kim:
And I'm wondering, Susan, where you got that "beginner's mind" or that thirst for learning from? If you cast your glance back to being a child, can you see yourself even in primary school, keen to learn something new?

Susan:
I am a learner. It's something I really enjoy doing. Even as recently as last week, I was looking at the possibility of enrolling in a master's degree course!

I went to quite a small country primary school, and in Year 5 the school agreed to integrate some children who had disabilities. Two younger girls were enrolled at our school – one had a physical and one had an intellectual disability. The teachers were upskilled and new infrastructure was added to the school to make the school "disability friendly."

The idea of integration into mainstream education seemed very new at the time in the early 1980s. At that stage, the senior students were asked to be mentors and companions to those young girls, and as an older student I found myself in that role. So, as I reflect back, I can see that I began my helping profession back in primary school, and that never wore off. Even during high school, I remember doing my Year 10 work experience at a Special Development School.

Kim:
I always find it intriguing when our careers have links to childhood experiences!

Susan:
When I completed Year 12, I thought I was either going to apply for kindergarten teaching or work in disability. I chose a course in Disability Studies and worked in that field for 20 years.

However, I always felt there was a missing part to the work I was doing with my clients who had a disability. I felt strongly there were many unmet needs for emotional support for the other family members who were supporting the person with a disability.

Ultimately, that's what led me to train as a counsellor.

Kim:
You were one of five children – did all of you move into caring, advocacy or counselling? And is there a connection there to your parents, too?

Susan:
Interestingly, four out of the five of us are in what I would consider to be helping professions. One sister is a senior lecturer in Occupational Therapy, another managed and worked in medical imaging and now she has moved to work in education and another is campus principal at a large country secondary school.

I remember as a little kid, Mum would be helping people who were living on their own in our small country town. Some didn't have enough food, and others had medical issues that needed to be tended to. My values around helping others very much came from my parents who did a lot of volunteering.

Kim:
And what kind of client groups have you been drawn to as a counsellor, Susan?

Susan:
I've worked with carers, people living with or surviving after domestic violence, and more recently I have been a grief and bereavement counsellor in community palliative care.

I have been growing my skills and confidence and I feel more comfortable in my profession as a counsellor, but I still experience that "imposter syndrome."

My colleagues, manager and clients say to me "you're an amazing counsellor" and "you're wonderful at your work," yet I'm continually surprised: "What? You're talking about me?" I have to stop and remind myself that what I do for a living is really making a difference, and that the individuals I work with are finding the work they're doing with me to be helpful.

I can get caught up in the everyday stress of the work and fail to recognise the value of the work I do. This interview gives me a beautiful opportunity to step back and notice that I am making a difference.

OUTSIDE MY COMFORT ZONE

I don't know if, because we're in the helping profession, we forget to stop and reflect on the work we do and the impact it has.

Making time to consider that my clients maybe did get to the place where they're at because of the work that we did together – that's really rewarding.

Kim:
Yes, this kind of self-affirmation and radical self-compassion is rare. When I first graduated, making time for reflective practice was considered just as important as attending a professional development seminar. It seems to have completely disappeared nowadays.

Susan:
One of the things that I know I struggled with during COVID-19 was the lack of informal opportunities to self-reflect with our team when working from home. Prior to the pandemic, we would have a meeting and acknowledge the deaths of clients in our service. Working in palliative care, we could have five to ten people die across a week. That meeting gave us a sacred time to stop and recognise all those

individuals, and the families who had lost a loved one that week. It was our time as a team to reflect on the work we had done.

Kim:
Can you share something that your clients have found helpful as they struggle with their grief?

Susan:
I sometimes say, "If I could meet you in a year's time, I know that things will be ok for you. I have learnt that time needs to pass, particularly when dealing with grief and loss, for things to be different. I don't know how the passing of time helps, or why, but I have learnt from my time as a counsellor in the palliative care and bereavement space, that in a year from now, you won't feel the way you do today."

I say, "I'm not saying it will hurt less. I'm not saying your life will be amazingly wonderful, but what I'm saying to you is when you look back at this first part of your grief experience, you'll be able to reflect on the passing of time and say, 'Yes, it is different now.' You might not even be able to say how, but you will be able to notice that it's different."

Kim:
It sounds like you were able to offer hope for change in the depths of a painful loss. What a sensitive way to express the journey with grief. And this isn't something you learnt at uni, but from life?

Susan:
Look, as you know Kim, following the sudden death of my own mum in my late 20s, I was fortunate enough to have a large, supportive family who provided the emotional support I needed at the time. Back then, I was unaware of professional bereavement counselling. What I noticed was that time was a great healer. I can't say when things changed, but a time came when I felt more able to cope without my mum. I somehow got to that place. I also know there are still days and special occasions when I feel her absence keenly.

On reflection, I do wonder if seeking professional support in my grief may have enabled me to navigate that challenging time in my life in a different way. As a counsellor, I've found that having a lived experience has meant supporting bereaved individuals is easier for me than I imagined it would be. I feel honoured to be there as they take the time to adjust to their new life without their loved one. The advice I share comes from my experience, but also from the collected wisdom of each and every bereaved individual I have supported.

Kim:
Life, and the clients we meet can teach us so much about what is helpful in counselling, Susan. What are some of the roles that stand out in these last seven years for you?

Susan:
Well, one of my last placements that I did as a student counsellor was with the Salvation Army in their alcohol and drug program. It was quite challenging and a massive learning curve. I had a really good supervisor who said, "You'll be ok!" and then he threw me in the deep end!

I found myself way outside my comfort zone. Working in drug and alcohol addiction services was a space that I knew nothing about, so I literally had to learn everything from scratch. That's been an interesting thing for me, that just about every job I've taken on, I've had little or no experience and I've learnt "on the job."

I came from a very sheltered life and upbringing, and the first thing I had to learn in that space was the different names and effects of all the drugs so I could understand people's drug history.

I clearly remember being interviewed for that placement by my supervisor. He said, "So tell me what you would do if a client came in for counselling and they presented maybe ten different issues. Where would you start?"

I recall saying, "I'd just start somewhere," literally because that was the first thing that came into my head at that time, and felt like common sense. Surprisingly he said, "That's exactly right." He said he tells students that people are like a messy ball of string or like a big bowl of pasta. You just need to pick a thread or a piece of spaghetti, and start somewhere.

> "Start now. Start where you are.
> Start with fear. Start with pain. Start with doubt.
> Start with hands shaking.
> Start with voice trembling but start. Start and don't stop.
> Start where you are, with what you have. Just... start."
> — IJEOMA UMEBINYUO

That's always stuck with me that fact that you start anywhere and eventually you'll figure out together the main reason for them seeking counselling support. Sometimes it takes a bit of time.

Working in drug and alcohol counselling taught me that a lot of the clients had experienced trauma, and that their lives were really complicated, and things felt out of their control. Many found that counselling helped them regain a sense of control and new perspectives about their lives.

My experience taught me to be really open to people from all different walks of life, with all different sorts of issues, and not to be afraid. I learnt that even though I had not wanted my placement to be in drug and alcohol counselling, I was able to learn that despite people's addictions and struggles, they were humans in pain seeking help and support. My main job was to connect with them as a human. It was invaluable for me to learn that as a student counsellor.

Kim:
What I'm hearing is that you weren't put off by the gap in your knowledge about the different drugs, or people who have had different

lifestyles. You are someone who loves to learn, you have that will to offer therapeutic support and you are capable of holding back on judgement.

Do you have more sparkling moments you'd like to share from your other part-time roles?

Susan:
For a few years, I have also facilitated group programs for separated parents. This has included providing education, counselling support and guidance to parents whose relationship and family unit has broken down. Working with parents who are learning how to co-parent their children has given me a fabulous opportunity to consider the different types of families, and the impact changes such as separation can have on parents and children. My work with separated parents also ties in nicely with the loss and grief work I do, because the emotional experiences whilst adjusting to a different family life often mirror the experience of bereavement.

I've worked as a contract counsellor in an Autism specific service, and I've done volunteer work at Uniting, where you were my supervisor. That was working with a wide variety of individuals from the community who were on the edge, with complex welfare needs and who couldn't financially afford to pay for counselling. At Uniting I was working with clients with significant long-term mental health issues, and trying to figure out how I could best support them. It was at that point in my counselling work that I started to understand that I can't fix people.

I had moved into counselling away from my previous role as a Disability Support case manager, where we could actively improve people's lives. As a counsellor, I had to step back from providing solutions. I had to keep reminding myself that my job is not to fix people's problems, and that no matter how much I wanted to help, no matter how troubled the clients might be, or how distressed I felt seeing them distressed, that the most important thing is to be present by listening, and being with the person. Being the best support that I can be at that time.

Last year, I did a course from the University of Tasmania on "Understanding Dementia." It was online and free. The knowledge I gained about dementia from that course has been invaluable because I'm currently working part-time as a counsellor in nursing homes, so how I approach those clients and also their families is now informed by that learning.

Kim:
Again, you follow your intuitions and opportunities in some interest area, and lo and behold, it turns out to be helpful knowledge for the next role!

Susan:
That's true. For a while I took on some project work at the Anxiety Recovery Centre of Victoria. I wasn't working as a counsellor there, but I learnt heaps about anxiety, which has been invaluable because anxiety is such a massive issue for many clients.

Then I helped run a support group for hoarders. I learnt that hoarding is a mental health condition and it's not simply people randomly collecting stuff. I saw individuals putting up their hand and saying, "I need some help and I'm not sure where to go."

After that, I took a part time role as a family violence counsellor. Which is so interesting, because if you'd asked me as a student, I would have said, "I'm not doing alcohol and other drug (AOD) counselling and I'm not doing domestic violence. Never, ever will I do those types of counselling! Too hard and too scary." Then, all of a sudden, I found myself having worked in both fields.

I was one of the contact workers for women who were currently or had previously experienced domestic violence. It was eye-opening and shocking for me to learn how common family violence was in the community, and how difficult the situation was for the women I spoke with.

Prior to coming into that job, my mindset around this problem was, "Why don't you leave?" Again, I was on this massive learning curve. The women I was working with were really trapped, and their children were trapped. I remember two separate women building up the strength and courage to leave, and how brave they needed to be to leave. They also spoke of how they found an opportunity to break the cycle of family violence that they'd been exposed to growing up.

I left my job in domestic violence because it was so difficult for me seeing people struggling with that choice to leave those relationships, but unable to do so, often because of the higher risk to women in the weeks after leaving. I got to a place professionally where I went, "I'm not doing my best work here, because I feel really stuck." At times, I also felt I lacked hope for these women and children.

When the clients felt really stuck, I felt really hopeless. That was one of the first times that I really noticed countertransference. I remember learning about this in my course, and back then I recall thinking, "Oh, what's this all about?" Then all of a sudden, there it was.

Kim:
I'm hearing how there can be wonderful moments in our work where we feel we have purpose, we've got something to offer. We may have compassion for a person's situation, affirm their strengths or hopes and we are being the best counsellor we can be. But then there can suddenly emerge a kind of undercurrent. There can be this dark energy that can just pull us down. There are days where we kind of go, "oh, I don't want to get up and do the job today."

So, I'm just wondering, are you able to relate to that?

Susan:
When I think about my role in the family violence space, after a while I lost the passion and connection to my purpose for doing this work. It came again in the last part of my current role in palliative care. I think my most recent disconnection was compounded by COVID-19 and the challenges in the general community.

I found things especially difficult working with families or individuals who didn't have a support network around them. Coming from a large family and from a small community where everyone knew one another, and where the community would make certain others were ok, I found seeing people who were isolated or alone very difficult.

In palliative care, families who had been bereaved during COVID-19 were alone, and many women who were in domestic violence situations were cut off from their family and friends by the perpetrator's coercive control. If I parallel those two roles and try to identify why they were challenging for me, it's the isolation that I saw in their lives that I struggled with. That drew me down into that dark undercurrent.

Kim:
As you share that, if you could put your hand on your belly or heart, where is it now?

Susan:
Feels like my heart's crunched up in this tiny black ball. I feel quite overwhelmed with that longing, that helplessness at seeing people alone. Our western culture values people being individualised and independent. However, as COVID-19 showed us, we need people and community, and we need people to draw together.

Kim:
And as you rightly said, that's countertransference when our own unmet needs and stress spills out into the therapeutic space. These confronting social dilemmas can contribute to our compassion fatigue and burnout. Whether we want to call it burnout, it doesn't really matter. We can know what it is, or sense what it feels like.

Susan:
It is frightening to me that counsellors talk about burnout in a blasé manner, like it is expected, almost a rite of passage. I've been confused by these attitudes, and I wonder why we aren't working harder to keep counsellors mentally well? Why are we waiting for them to crash before we pick them up and dust them off, and say, "You'll be ok. Keep doing the good work." How do we get to that place?

Kim:
This is the missing piece of the puzzle, of what it takes to support a team of people doing this counselling work. You know, back in the day, Susan, I used to work at a place called Women's Health West. They had a budget for the child counselling team to go away for our self-care each year. We once went to the Mornington Peninsula Hot Springs. We sat and chatted and laughed in the spa, and were paid to relax and reconnect. And that was prioritised in the team's wellbeing budget.

Susan:
We do need time together to rest and recuperate in these roles.

Kim:
Yes, making time for those conversations. Creating a culture where colleagues, managers or supervisors say, "let's catch up for a coffee." It can happen if it is supported from top-down.

I recall at the Western Region Health Centre (now CoHealth) they had this kind of "people are important" philosophy. Every morning tea, the team would walk up to a café in Barkly Street and sit down for coffee and a chat. Then, once a week on a Wednesday, close to our lunchtime, there was a ukulele club, and we jammed away with great enthusiasm in a room adjoining the waiting area at this multidisciplinary building. And we'd practise all these corny songs, you know, Beatles, ABBA, romantic ballads and pop tunes. There was lots of laughter, as nobody was particularly musical! And when all these counsellors with their little ukuleles left the room, people in the waiting area who were there to see their doctors and dentists, would all give us a round of applause! All that laughter and singing must have been the perfect antidote to stress. Only later did I see all the research about long exhalations being great for mind-body health and reducing the effects of trauma.

The CEO, whose room was adjoining ours upstairs, would also join us most days for a three-minute spontaneous dance opportunity! Someone would put on a YouTube music video, (people placed their requests) and we'd call down the corridor, "dance party!" and soon the room was crowded with us all dancing merrily for the three minutes of that song. That special fun time of coming together didn't even need a budget. It was such a beautiful, warm workplace.

Susan:
I agree there is a need to create more opportunities for fun and joy.

Kim:
You have moved into private practice now, and are pondering doing the master's. What else is on the cards?

Susan:

A while ago I completed some family therapy studies, which is now proving helpful with families I see. I am interested in learning more about narrative therapy and emotion focused therapy (EFT) too.

Kim:

You certainly have that zest for learning, Susan. Have any particular modalities been valuable in your work?

Susan:

The Acceptance and Commitment Therapy (ACT) framework is about saying, "Well, this is what's happened, but I can choose what's next." Every day is a series of choices, and we make those decisions, and it's ok if we change our minds at any time. There are no wrong decisions.

Kim:

It sounds like you find ways to awaken people to an understanding that we do have choices, and again, we wouldn't judge them if they deferred making choices, that's ok. Even not making a choice is making a choice.

Susan:

I've also learnt over time to integrate all the knowledge and skills I have gathered along the way. I remember right at the end of my counselling course being told, "Most counsellors will have an eclectic style of counselling." At the time I didn't really know what that meant, or how I could possibly integrate all the different theories and styles I was being taught! However, recently a new colleague asked me, "What counselling frameworks do you use? What theories do you use?"

Funnily enough when I answered, I found myself describing my work as "quite eclectic!"

Kim:
That's such a wonderful discovery. I'm laughing at the way we can never quite predict what direction we will take in the future. Thanks so much for our conversation today, Susan.

Bio:

Susan lives with her husband, Theo, two children, Zoe and Archer, and their westie, Hudson, in Southeast Melbourne. Susan grew up on a dairy farm outside Oxley in Northeast Victoria. When she is not working, Susan enjoys reading, running, connecting with nature and spending time with family and friends.

Website: skcounselling.com.au

Qualifications:
Counsellor. BA (Disability Studies), Grad. Dip Coaching & Counselling, M.A.C.A.

CHAPTER 5

Finding the Rainbow Connection
with Pamela Cox

Kim:
Welcome, Pamela. I wonder which words you'd prefer me or other counsellors to use, when referring to the LGBTQIA+ community: people who identify under that lovely rainbow umbrella?

Pamela:
Well, instead of using the alphabet soup, I just say the Rainbow Community, and that's quite a common sort of shortcut.

Kim:
I love that! What age were you when you began to notice people identifying differently from the two genders that are presented in our culture?

Pamela:

In my adolescent years, I realised that my behaviour was different to my peer group. I wasn't "boy mad," I didn't chase after boys or seek to have a boyfriend. I found myself attracted to girls. I did some research and started reading lots of psychology books and to my horror realised this was defined as a mental illness. And I thought, right, no one's going to tell me I have a mental illness! I may belong to a minority group as such, but I'm not mentally ill.

Kim:

So much was going on for you. How amazing you found that information, Pamela.

Pamela:

I probably found it in an early edition of the DSM back in the 60s, and it wasn't removed completely until the 1980s as a mental illness. And, of course, in some countries it remains a crime. So, I decided that I was going to become a professional and provide counselling to people where they didn't have to explain themselves to me and I didn't treat them as having a mental illness because of their sexuality or lifestyle choices.

Kim:

It feels like the challenges never quite go away?

Pamela:

One of the first and most difficult challenges is "coming out:" first to yourself, then to the wider community.

The process of coming out is never something that you do once; you do it your whole life. Unless you live in a cocoon or are completely "in the closet," there is barely a week that passes that I might be asked something like, "What about your husband, what does he do?" Depending on the circumstances I have to make a decision to come out, or answer in gender neutral language.

Kim:
These normative assumptions that the culture has about every human being are such a burden.

Pamela:
Yeah, and it's different to race or ethnicity, or people from culturally and linguistically diverse (CALD) backgrounds which are usually more obvious. So, sometimes people are poised to make choices about, "Will I be out here?" And the anxiety can be quite profound, and some people never completely get out of the closet. You know, they might have one foot in the closet, one foot out.

Kim:
So you're making daily decisions, depending on how safe it is to be open about something? Who was the first person who you could share anything about this with, even in a small degree?

Pamela:
I was 18 years old and it was a cousin who's two years younger than me. He didn't have any negative reaction. It didn't affect my relationship

with him. He is very supportive and caring toward me and my partner to this day.

Kim:
What was it like for you, when the first person that you discuss this with, said it was all ok? It was very natural. What was that like for you?

Pamela:
I guess I was waiting for some kind of reaction, because at the time, his life involved being in a bikie club, but he just said, "Yeah, ok." It was a relief to be accepted for who I was, and not who I might form relationships with.

Coming out to him became a catalyst for me to find my own path. I left home, quit my pharmacy degree and set out to make my way in the world.

> "There's power in allowing yourself to be known and heard.
> In owning your unique story.
> In using your authentic voice."
> — MICHELLE OBAMA

Kim:
So, you're out there, left home and university and started working. Were you able to be a little bit more of yourself?

Pamela:
Yeah, definitely. Back then finding "community" was complex. I was living around the inner suburbs of Melbourne in a flat in Windsor, with a lot of the community around Elwood, St Kilda, Balaclava etc. I was sharing with a friend from school who was very accepting.

Finding suitable work was challenging but fortunately I secured a position in the public service where staff were encouraged to undertake further studies. I was placed in the PMG (which later became Australia Post) in the accounting department – which nearly drove me crazy, but I was glad to have a secure job which enabled me to support myself.

I was working full-time and undertaking my first degree in psychology part-time. It was a dead boring job during the day, but it enabled me to find the capacity to do something that I was passionate about at night school; sometimes sitting up studying to two or three in the morning, trying to finish assignments and still going to work the next day.

Kim:
After graduation, how did your career start to take shape?

Pamela:
As I was approaching the completion of my degree, I was fortunate enough to secure work in the Human Services department of the PMG. I held many positions in that department including Equal Opportunity Officer, Senior Recruitment Officer and Psychologist undertaking research into aptitude testing. Back then the PMG also had a welfare section which provided counselling to all staff working in Victoria.

When I saw a vacancy for a Welfare Officer position, I applied and was successful, and although I took a drop in pay to transfer into that role, that fulfilled my aspirations and passion.

Kim:
So, as a qualified psychologist, were doors opening for you?

Pamela:
The experiences I acquired in Australia Post really launched my professional career. I was a Senior Counsellor at the time of the 1987 Queen Street shootings and was seconded into a Trauma and Recovery Team. I learnt so much during that intensely difficult time.

I left Australia Post after 19 years' service. At the time, I was Manager of Employee Assistance with responsibility for 13 counsellors and two administrative staff. Being a manager was ok but took me away from counselling. I decided it was time for me to change direction and seek work in a community setting.

The first position I secured was a locum as a sexual assault counsellor at the Northern East Centre Against Sexual Assault, or NECASA, but that was only for a few months to fill a maternity leave position.

After leaving NECASA, I became despondent as I struggled to find another counselling position despite numerous applications. I started to believe I was possibly over-qualified. Finally, I secured a position with the Victorian Aids Council (VAC) and the Gay Men's Health Centre (GMHC); I had found my rainbow connection.

It was such a unique environment, like stepping into another world. Most of the staff were from the rainbow community as were a significant number of the clients. I was the only female psychologist working alongside three male psychologists. It was a bizarre transition, because I'd come from a feminist environment at CASA with lots of posters of women's empowerment, and I walked into the Gay Men's Health Centre, with images of gay men's empowerment. And I went, "Oh, ok, this is an adjustment." And I thought, "How will the men relate to me as a woman?" I was immediately welcomed as a sister in the rainbow community. In the end, I had a long waiting list as many of the men felt more comfortable with a female counsellor. And it was an absolute pleasure and a privilege to work with them. It was like walking into another world where being gay, lesbian or whatever was normal.

Kim:
You found a welcoming space?

Pamela:
Yeah, and it was more than that. It was just feeling like you're in a space where everything's normal, you know, no one questions you, and you could just be yourself.

Kim:
I'm hearing how this passion evolved and you became someone who can make a difference with people in your community, through this counselling and psychology career. That passion also sounds like it helped you get through the challenges of belonging to a minority group?

Pamela:
I was determined to get through my qualifications and training to ensure I could work with my community.

> "Your time is limited so don't waste it living someone else's life.
> Don't be trapped by dogma which is living someone else's life."
> — STEVE JOBS

Kim:
Would you like to share some stories from the next phase of your career?

Pamela:
I secured another position as a sexual assault counsellor at WestCASA which I enjoyed immensely as the women were such competent counsellors and functioned as a team. One counsellor spoke of a job she was leaving in community health, and this was my next stroke of good luck. I was successful in filling her vacancy and became a counsellor at Craigieburn Community Health Centre, which later merged with the Broadmeadows Community Health to become Dianella Community Health. I worked with a great diversity of professionals including social workers, youth workers, doctors, OTs, physios, nurses and workers supporting refugees.

A big part of my role in community health was not just counselling but community development/education and running groups.

I worked closely with the Broadmeadows Community Legal Service and participated in a network of family violence workers.

I also had the opportunity to run an internship program with the Master of Counselling Psychology department from La Trobe University. As well as mentoring the interns in counselling techniques, we ran therapeutic and educational groups. These included postnatal depression groups, depression groups, family violence etc. but we gave them special names to hide what they were about because of shame and stigma.

I worked three and a half days a week in community health as well as conducting a part-time private practice which I established after leaving Australia Post. In 2010, after 17 years, I left community health and continued with my private practice.

Not long after leaving Dianella Community Health, another opportunity arose. I was headhunted to work part-time as a psychologist at Prahran Market GP Clinic. It was like revisiting the VAC/GMHC experience in the 1990s; a clinic where most of the staff and many of the patients belonged to the "community."

Returning to work in the rainbow community nearly 30 years later, so much had changed in the treatment of HIV; unlike at VAC in the 1980s where people were dying of AIDs, these clients were well, and had been living with HIV for two and three decades.

I felt very fortunate to have the opportunity to work with my community again. Unlike VAC/GMHC, this clinic also provided services to women from the rainbow community, and I was able to provide counselling to lesbian women.

Kim:
Having such a long career, you could have got close to burnout, which is what can happen?

Pamela:
Retrospectively, I think the diversity of activities and opportunities that community health provided kept burnout at bay.

However, I was greatly saddened to learn that one very bright young intern of mine left community health and started working pretty much full-time doing private practice, and burnt out within a few years.

I also saw the stress in CASA counsellors who worked for years in sexual assault and the impact it had on their lives both personally and professionally; burnout was never far away.

I think one of the secrets of longevity is being able to do a variety of activities. For example, whilst working at VAC, I was also the coordinator of the Red Ribbon Project.

Kim:
And what was the Red Ribbon Project, Pamela? I don't recall that one.

Pamela:
People would sell red ribbons and raise money because, back in those days, there wasn't any money available for the medications and treatment that HIV positive people needed. The men were so good, so creative, like one very talented man created these amazing teddy bears. He'd sew little costumes and dress up these teddy bears brilliantly as Marilyn Monroe, Elizabeth Taylor and Elvis and so on, and they would be auctioned and raised thousands of dollars.

There were a lot of volunteer hours outside of normal working hours, but there were trade-offs, like my partner and I got tickets to go and see the movie *Philadelphia* and attend an Elton John concert!

Kim:
What are some of the key issues which have been challenging along the way?

Pamela:
You're probably aware that the incidence of psychological distress and risk of suicide is greater in the "community," but much of that comes from a lack of acceptance and alienation. Unlike other minority groups, the key word here is sex, and western societies and lots of others tend to get hung up about sex. No one approaches a heterosexual person wanting to know how they discovered their sexual preference or identity. And this is something that people get very hung up on.

Kim:
What could you share that may help counsellors with clients who identify as non-binary and so on?

Pamela:
What is little understood is that people from the "community" mostly come to counselling not to talk about their sexuality, but for all the usual issues to do with depression, relationships, anxiety and so on. Then there may be issues around "internalised homophobia," which is a lack of self-acceptance, or rejection by one's family of origin relating to their gender identity.

So instead of me cross-examining them about, "when do you think you became gay?" and "are you certain about this?" and "how were you treated as a child?" You know, immediately the defences go up! Whereas for me, I say, "Ok. So, let's talk about what has brought you to counselling; what are the issues that are troubling you?"

I have also developed a theory that our learning about being in relationships tends to be a little bit delayed. Whilst most people in the larger society are busy exploring their heterosexual relationships in their adolescent years, the exploration of relationships can get delayed when there's a cultural and societal lack of acceptance of other non-heterosexual relationships. So, for some from the "community," they may persevere, trying to lead a life that is acceptable, and don't come out until much later in life, sometimes after being married and having children.

Kim:
And where are you at now?

Pamela:
Now I'm in transition to retirement, after 45 years of counselling. I certainly never imagined I'd be doing this for as long as I have.

Kim:
I have loved our interview today and learnt so much, Pamela. Thanks for sharing stories about your many years of experiences and your passion for this work. Have you any last reflections?

Pamela:
Well, I often think about empowerment. I try and reduce the power imbalance that is evident in the therapeutic relationship. That's key to what I do. I describe myself as a travelling companion with my clients. We might reach a fork in the road, and they're trying to decide whether to go left or right. So, we talk about it.

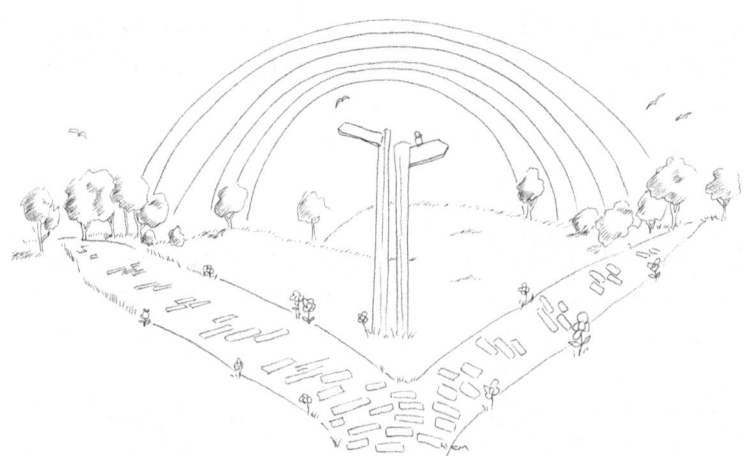

At other times, I might say to my clients, "If you think I've got the answers, well, you've come to the wrong person! But together we can explore the possibilities and seek some healing outcomes."

And, sometimes people ask me, "How come you got into psychology?" And I don't want to sound religious or anything, but it was a bit like a calling to do it, you know? To realise that's where my strengths lie, and to use them to try and make a difference in people's lives.

Into the future, I will be keen to see what difference the changes to the Marriage Act make for young members of the rainbow community, growing up with that endorsement of their relationships. I know from a personal perspective that the changes lock in legal rights, such as next of kin, that were not previously recognised. I hope these changes will lead to less discrimination and greater acceptance of non-traditional relationships. It is one step on a long road toward inclusion and equality. I can include a case study that may help others understand these complexities.

Case Study

Amanda* is a 48-year-old lesbian woman who was initially referred to counselling for depression and anxiety following a back injury after a fall in an aged care facility where she worked as a carer.

What unfolded through the course of our sessions was that Amanda's partner had given birth to a baby boy. As Amanda was off work recovering, she became the full-time carer of their son, Adam. Her partner returned to studies and nursing.

After three and a half years, their relationship broke down and the separation was acrimonious.

Despite Amanda being recorded as a parent on Adam's birth certificate, her ex stopped her from seeing and communicating with Adam. Adam was now six years old, and he used to call Amanda "mama."

Amanda fought to have contact with Adam. She described them as having a strong bond and being very close. She tried to take legal action, but due to the high costs, she was not successful.

Amanda said when she was 17 years old and first came out to her parents, she was ordered out of the house. She had worked hard to repair her relationship with her parents, but their approach to her current situation was that she should "stop trying to have contact with Adam... after all, he's not really your son..." Amanda felt alone through this time, in despair and at times felt like giving up on life.

*Names have been changed

Bio:

Pamela was born in Melbourne in 1950 and spent her early years in "working class" Fitzroy. Her parents received an allocation of land as they had served in the forces during World War II and the family moved to "country" Watsonia in 1957.

Pamela and Yvonne, her partner of 40 years, lived in a quaint log cabin in Hurstbridge for over 30 years but now reside near Tara Bulga National Park in Gippsland with their "fur" family: Tara, a toy poodle and Bonny, a west highland terrier.

They are passionate about the environment, the local wildlife and gardening, which involves caring for many native plants, over 70 roses and 22 fruit trees.

Qualifications:

Pamela is a registered psychologist, and a Fellow of the College of Counselling Psychologists. Bachelor of Arts (Psych); Graduate Diploma of Counselling; Master of Arts (Women's Studies).

Member of the Australian Psychological Society (MAPS) Fellow of Counselling College of MAPS

CHAPTER 6

Evolution Not Revolution: The Challenge of Simple, Hard Work

with Tom Lothian

Kim:
Thanks for coming today, Tom. What were you doing before you became a mature-age psychology student?

Tom:
I was an accountant before I was a psychologist. Psychology wasn't on my radar when I was 18 and coming out of high school. Even if it had been, I don't think I was ready to start heading in that direction. So, I was casting around for different things that I could have done. I initially thought I wanted to be a medical doctor and happily I fell short of the marks required. I ended up in a commerce degree.

Halfway through that degree, I realised that I didn't want to be an accountant, but I didn't have a better plan, so I toughed it out and completed the degree.

In the final year, I met a psychologist through a personal connection, and as I was having conversations with him it struck me that this would be a job that plays to a lot of my strengths, but also appeals to my values a lot more than my accounting degree.

I graduated with very poor marks because I was not a dedicated accounting student, and secured a graduate job where I worked for four years.

Then six months after finishing university, I was back studying psychology part-time while I worked full-time. While I had very little time off between the first and second degrees, I came to the second degree with a completely different mentality. Part of it was the old adage, if you want something done, give it to a busy person. Part of it was that I found the study absolutely fascinating.

That was a pretty full on three years doing the psych undergrad while working full time. It was a very energy intensive experience.

Kim:
So, you're in your 20s and travelling light?

Tom:
Less responsibility and complexity back then. No kids, a job I enjoyed, all care and minimal responsibility. I'd almost entirely covered statistics in my accounting degree, which allowed me the time and space to then pour all this energy into winning the competition of undergraduate psychology.

Sadly, in undergraduate psychology courses, it's a behavioural science trivia competition. The competition filters the thousands of people who enter first year psychology down to the 60 who will enter fourth year psychology. And you can't become a psychologist without getting into that fourth year.

I don't want to disparage the knowledge you acquire in undergraduate psychology. There's a lot of foundational information of the profession that has served me well as a therapist.

Kim:
I see a lot of students coming through the Master of Counselling course who say, "Oh, my first degree is in psychology." So maybe when they didn't hit that top mark, counselling became plan B?

Tom:
Right. And I think importantly, the nature of that system has now selected a cohort, a whole generation of psychologists, who are highly perfectionistic and very obsessive because that's what's required in order to get into the postgraduate qualification. I think that's an important selective pressure to call out because it leaves the profession with certain blind spots. I think it's great for psychologists to look at their own sensitivities, like the OCD-flavoured perfectionistic stuff. That's a big issue for almost all psychologists.

Kim:
That's a great observation, Tom. And I'm interested, if when you're providing supervision, do you sometimes meander a little bit into this topic? Obviously, you can refer your supervisees to go and get some counselling around these issues, but do you sometimes find yourself unpacking the supervisee's own in-session reactions and history?

Tom:
Oh, absolutely. I have a tendency to follow the Daphne Hewson school of supervision. Daphne, who notably is not a psychologist, encourages discussion of anything connected to the work. You don't have to unpack that stuff in supervision, but you can. You do need to unpack it somewhere, otherwise it's going to get in the way of your therapy practice.

I think that the conversations where there is an overlap between therapy and supervision speaks to the different ways we can all be reactive as clinicians, and that being reactive is allowed.

Sometimes you don't know what you're talking about in the therapy with your client until later. You often need hindsight to reflect on some work with a client and say, "oh, I can see that the last six months was spent working on trust, because now you're ready to take off that armour and reveal to me that you have an underlying history of attachment problems. (See illustrations next page) So, while I was a bit uncertain as to what we were discussing at the time, I knew it was meaningful because there was emotion in the room." I think that pattern can play out in supervision as well.

Kim:
That reminds me of how the presenting "issue" often conceals a more central issue which is hidden until trust develops. These conversations are so interesting, Tom. Tell me more about your earlier workplaces.

Tom:
My formative experience as a therapist was spent working in a drug and alcohol unit in a prison where there was a very intensive supervision process: an hour of group and an hour of individual each week. After three years in that job, I realised that I'd just spent three years talking about my insecurities, even though I hadn't directly raised them.

I'd been working on insecurities because if I can change my reactivity to my insecurities, I can hold more emotional space in the session. In simple terms, holding emotional space is about allowing another person to be emotional, while you are both emotional and calm. Someone needs to be holding the space in any given conversation. In the context of therapy, the clinician has always got to have their stuff managed so they can be emotionally connected and stay calm.

EVOLUTION NOT REVOLUTION: THE CHALLENGE OF SIMPLE, HARD WORK

Kim:
I like the way you talk about this noticing of reactivity, because it's going to happen. Eugene Gendlin says when he goes into the session, he puts all his own stuff on one side of himself, and acknowledges he might need it, and after this, he aims to be fully present.

Tom:
We sometimes describe reactivity as countertransference, when the client's experience resonates with your own experience you will have a stronger emotional reaction. There are some advantages to strong countertransferences. Your emotional system is being tapped louder so you'll get to the punchline a lot faster than a clinician who doesn't have that history. The downside is that having emotions is an energetic process. So, it can be easier to exhaust yourself if you're using your emotions to inform the therapy. Which comes back to a lot of the themes that I work with in my own supervision and the supervision of others.

You've got to be prepared to not do too much deep empathy otherwise you'll exhaust yourself. Perfectionistic, obsessive clinicians love nothing more than working themselves into the ground. We have a tendency as a tribe to be very self-sacrificing as well. Unfortunately, this can be highly destructive. Particularly if you're working in the complex trauma space.

Kim:
And it sounds like you have some inside information about this topic. So, I'm just wondering if someone from your childhood were listening to us today, would they be going, "You know, Tom is the perfect person to work with complex cases?"

Tom:
Sometimes I describe my work to other people in my life and they shake their heads and say, "There's zero chance I could ever do that." I always challenge that and say, "my work is absolutely accessible to you. It would require enormous quantities of very painful, often

EVOLUTION NOT REVOLUTION: THE CHALLENGE OF SIMPLE, HARD WORK

confusing work, so you're going to choose not to, and that's an entirely sensible choice." I think doing this work is accessible to anyone who wants to do it.

For me, the choice to do the work is more important than the strengths and weaknesses that you have at the start.

Kim:
And are you guided by gut feelings?

Tom:
Absolutely. For me, the gut reactions are the emotional process. The brain and neural cells are distributed through the entire body. So, I think we are always perceiving the world in two different ways: the emotional system and the rational system. These systems don't need to agree with each other. One of the downsides of the emotional system is that it doesn't use its words. It will give you a feeling or an impulse or a twinge. Sometimes you can interpret that. Sometimes you know something's there, and it takes a long time to figure out what that was. And sometimes you never get a handle on it because it was too subtle.

Kim:
When I first met you, I saw this authenticity and confidence you had about your clinical approaches and as a deep thinker, as well as your "quirky" self. You probably never said that, but you know what I'm saying?

Tom:
Oh, I'm a total weirdo and quite comfortable with that.

Growing up, being weird was part of me. I came to the realisation at some point that there's no point in fighting weirdness. The problem was caring about other people judging that. Which leads me to the most complex thing I ever discuss in therapy.

EVOLUTION NOT REVOLUTION: THE CHALLENGE OF SIMPLE, HARD WORK

If you let yourself be who you are, then finding the tribe of people where you fit in is an important part of life. You can try and change yourself to fit the expectations of others, but that is not as attractive an option as finding your social circle.

Kim:
In this work, you help people identify the origin of wounds, the protective armour created for safety, the barriers for them to move forward on their own and what works for them. But some people don't even get this far because there can be a stigma about reaching out.

Tom:
Definitely, we still have lots of work to do on the stigma of mental health issues. My aim is always to have folks see counselling as not meaningfully different from physiotherapy. The jobs are actually remarkably similar. Physiotherapists will tell you what's going on inside. Like in your knee. And then a physiotherapist will give you a set of exercises and stretches to do, which will be hard and boring and you don't want to do them. And then if you do them you get better. And if you don't do them, you don't.

Ultimately, one job of a therapist is to make yourself redundant in the client's life as quickly as you possibly can. One of the challenges is that the clinician has almost no control because it's the client who has the answers and the client who does the work, it's mostly the client already having the answers.

My experience is that the work is typically really simple, and really, really hard. If we frame it up as hard work then that's fine because we can pace ourselves. We can deal with any quantity of pain, as long as you spread it out over enough time. That's why my dominant metaphor of therapy is marathon training.

Kim:
Yes. I wondered, is that metaphor there because you have inside knowledge about running marathons?

Tom:
Yeah, I've done some of the pretty long runs. The reason I like it as a metaphor is because everyone knows how to run. It's left foot, right foot, repeat. It's not a complicated process. The hard bit is doing it.

Kim:
And the meaning-making of the hard work of therapy is part of what we talk about.

Tom:
Yes, to start to really be curious about your pain, which is pretty full on as a process. To loop back to the start of this conversation around how the clinician engages the client to get a deep history. Different clinicians do that in different ways. Personally, I let the client unravel that history at their pace. The only topics where I'm really insistent on getting to that conversation faster than the client might want to are immediate risk problems. The client can't get better if they're dead, is the simple wisdom of my particular flavour of therapy. If death is going to get in the way of therapy, that is going to be at the top of the agenda, but as far as disclosing their history, I let clients do that at their own pace.

Kim:
And if they trust that connection, then it's not going to be as overwhelming.

Tom:
And also to reinforce that the client is in charge of this therapy. My job is not to do the work for them. Not because I'm unwilling. I would love to be able to do the work for them. That's the obsessive, self-sacrificing part of me. However, I've got all the power and none of the control; I can't force happiness and wellbeing into anyone. That's magic. And no one in the history of my profession has ever solved that problem.

Kim:
Would you say magic sometimes happens in the sessions? I use that word liberally, but I wonder about your take on all this? I've

EVOLUTION NOT REVOLUTION: THE CHALLENGE OF SIMPLE, HARD WORK

known you for a few years and I know you used to work a lot with families and teenagers. Again and again, people came out of a series of sessions with you, looking radiant and with a different way of looking at their lives. A different confidence, a different capacity to tolerate things. And so, although you might say, "Oh, well, anyone could do it," it feels like magic happens around you with the choices you make around being with your clients. You make sure the client knows they're doing the work, you know, and it can all come together wonderfully in the end.

Tom:
I think to describe it as magic in that way? Sure, and I would love to call it magic. It's just that it's such hard work. If I think about the long therapy relationships that I've had, it was so hard. The clients, they get to the end of the therapy work hardened, sensitive, gritty, beautiful beings. They are so expert in pain and toughness at the same time. I don't think you can be brave unless you are afraid. I think it's your emotion that defines the hardness.

That's why I don't think of therapy as magical. In the sense that two people come together and they create a change where none has existed for a long time? I see the temptation in calling that magic, but it's so much work and so much effort. It requires a bloody-minded stubbornness on the client's behalf, and sometimes on my behalf, to hang in there, despite all of the odds telling us that this is a terrible idea and then choosing to do it anyway.

That's the thing that I find so rewarding about my job, watching people turn themselves inside out in the most positive way. Very slowly, over long periods of time and to be brave and tough and sensitive and connected all at the same time.

Kim:
These amazing clients are like our professors. They teach us everything we need to know. How is it for your clients, when that penny drops?

Tom:
The penny has to drop in a couple of different ways, rationally and emotionally. Rationally? First session, no worries. Because rational change is easy. Rational change is what we usually describe as changing your mind. I rationally change my mind all the time. New science comes out, or I'm having an interesting conversation with a client and I learn new things about their specific cultural background. And I can change my mind; it's no harder than clicking my fingers.

Changing emotional minds? That is hard. That is repetitive practise until you no longer respond in the way that you used to. In cognitive behavioural therapy we call it exposure therapy. If you turn up to therapy with a fear of spiders, then you practise triggering that anxiety again and again and again, until you no longer react with anxiety. That's tiring and scary.

I think the downside of exposure as it has been practised, is that the full context is often missing. So, sometimes a client presents with a fear of spiders. That's on the surface, but if your fear of spiders is tied into a fear of being out of control or feeling threatened, and it turns out that those feelings are grounded in a history of childhood family violence, then when you're doing your anxiety work for spiders, you're also doing deep trauma work. That's a very different context. So the work will go slower, but the work will go slower because the work has got more tied to it.

Hearing the full context of what the work really means to each client is really important. Letting that penny drop, that this guy called Tom is not coming to save me. I have clients where we lay that out in the first session and then we talk about it for five years.

Because the client knows it, but the client doesn't feel it yet. Because if I'm not in charge, that means the client has to be in charge. And that can be very attractive and also very confronting.

My work is all about when clients think one thing and feel another. Then we work on allowing ourselves to be internally contradictory. We change our rational mind when we need to, and we shape our emotional minds when we need to. That's as true of the client as it is of the clinician. I feel confident in my knowledge and comfortable with myself. I also feel like an imposter, because why would I be the specific individual who can facilitate change? I'm very confident in my lack of magic. I think I have adequate mental capacity, but I know I'm not a genius.

Kim:
You have many years' experience and training with what we sometimes call 'the pointy end' of the more challenging and complex issues. As a clinician you make choices and prioritise things that work for you. And that's what I've always liked about you Tom. You seem to have that confidence to know that 'this works for me' and you don't have to explain it, though today you have been explaining these things exquisitely! Thank you so much for sharing your insights and practice wisdom today, Tom.

Tom:
Thanks. I think really importantly, there's no one way to be a therapist. I do the therapy the way I do it because it works for me. There's no point in me turning up and trying to be you, Kim. In fact, you and I are a great example of very contrasting styles. You have colour and movement and tools – I mean, walking into your child therapy room was like Santa's workshop. An amazing space.

Whereas my therapy room has very little going on. I have a little bit of colour to stop it from being sterile, but there's not much there because I take more of a blank slate approach. I want the client to project and push what they want into the space. So, I bring my personality, but I boundary off a lot of my personal history.

It's the reason why I don't have my pronouns on my email. It's not because I'm against that as a concept, I'm very in favour of people feeling good about themselves, irrespective of gender and sex. The reason I don't is because I want to leave clients the space to assume that I'm gay or straight or non-binary or whatever they need me to be.

Bio:

Tom is a clinical psychologist and has worked with clients from ages four to 80 in a wide range of settings. He has experience in psychiatric hospitals, private practice, community drug and alcohol, community health and working in the adult forensic system. In addition to individual, couples and group therapy Tom is an experienced trainer and developer of therapeutic and training manuals. He has worked with clients on a variety of challenges including trauma, substance use, anxiety, depression, eating disorders, personality disorders, gender and sexual issues, anger and offending, and social skills for clients on the autism spectrum. Tom finds his work mostly fun and always rewarding.

Ph: 0400 341 940
Fax: 03 6146 1789
Website: https://www.therapypeople.com.au

Qualifications:
Clinical Psychologist

CHAPTER 7

It's Never Too Late…
For Secure Relationships
to Blossom and Grow
with Robyn Ball

Kim:
Welcome, Robyn. We share a similar passion for the wellbeing of children. Tell me about your own childhood journey and the connections to the work you do now with the Circle of Security.

Robyn:
I'm from a large Irish family and my parents immigrated here in 1959. I remember being fascinated by my heavily pregnant Auntie Iris, and then months later sitting beside my baby cousin Colin, and rocking him in his bassinet. My mum's younger sister, Emma was a midwife and I wanted to be a midwife when I grew up too! I've always loved being in the presence of babies.

Kim:
That is a picture of love! It sounds as though there were people who maybe already knew back then that you may well be doing this kind of work with parents and babies? Would they be saying, "Well of course, Robyn ends up doing this work!"

Robyn:
Yes, and it's been a journey! The world of infant mental health opened up for me in 2010 when I started work in a local children's centre and attended infant mental health consults every fortnight. I got to see that each baby has their own unique mind and needs within their family and community. We can learn a lot from babies' behaviours when we slow down and listen

Kim:
Many years ago, I remember hearing the term "infant mental health" and thinking, "what are they talking about?" Then I had a six-month student placement at a Mother and Baby Unit, at a psychiatric hospital who were using the "still face" studies to assess attachment problems. I previously pictured mental health as being something that was more to do with adolescents or adults. Research now shows that infants mental wellbeing is affected by the social environment around them, and meeting their emotional needs allows for a trajectory of healthy, neurological growth. I was amazed to learn how the social brain is developing rapidly during the baby's first thousand days.

Robyn:
Yes, in these first 1,000 days and especially the first 100 days, we are learning more and more about how the quality of calm and sensitive care and relationships provide the best environment for optimal human development.

Through attuned adult responses to infants in these early days, positive brain pathways connect and strengthen to form the building blocks for developing responsive stress systems that can help a child deal well with challenges that inevitably arise in life.

Kim:
So, resilience trajectories start very early. I'm a bit curious. Do you think that your birth order or other things in your family of origin enabled you to have an experience of that healthy mental and social development yourself, as a lived experience? Or do you feel you've kind of gone into this field because you might not have had that?

Robyn:
I am a middle child and the emotional challenges I've had growing up have led me into this field of early development. The Circle of Security course has helped me understand my own emotions and attachment history, and I'm now able to sit with that, and continue to become a better parent and grandparent.

I learnt that blame is a dead-end street, and that all parents want the best for their kids and that we are all on a journey of "becoming."

Kim:
That is so true, and once we become parents and see ourselves falling into intergenerational patterns, that is often a wake-up call.

Robyn:
We've all had unmet needs as children, and things happened that weren't right, and we didn't get things that would have been helpful to us.

I'm interested in how we can build confidence in ourselves as parents, to be open with our children in working towards balance, and knowing that when we make mistakes, it is actually the repair process that builds secure attachment relationships with our children.

Kim:
Most counsellors and the parents we work with won't have had some kind of perfect, rosy childhood. We all have some lived experience of these kinds of difficulties.

Robyn:

Yes, we can't turn back the clock. And anyway, there is nothing to fix. Walking alongside, listening, sharing and contributing to each other's lives, strengthens our relationships along the ups and downs that we all face in our lives.

Kim:

In what ways does this Circle of Security approach help parents?

Robyn:

I have found it to be a fabulous program that has been well researched and offers many "aha" moments where parents get to see things from a new perspective. Even their child's meltdowns become fabulous learning moments – now that is a gift!

Kim:

Recognising the child's needs is more than changing a wet nappy or providing food. How do you explain the Circle of Security to new families you're working with?

Robyn:

The program aims to increase a parent's confidence and teaches them how to become a secure emotional base for their child. This involves learning how to interpret the child's behaviours and what they may be feeling and needing, rather than attaching an often negative interpretation about what a child does. For example, a parent initially may think, "the child is manipulating me," or "they just want attention." The Circle of Security uses a simple circle graphic of coming and going, and video examples to show that all behaviour is communication.

Kim:
All behaviour is communication. That's such an important lens.

Robyn:
Yes, and there are feelings and needs underneath all behaviours, so it can be very confusing for parents to respond with wisdom to their children's behaviours!

I have a story of a young mum who after Week 1 of the course, said, "Robyn, this Circle of Security has already changed so much. It is amazing already. Now when Amy comes back in, she just wants to check in with me for a second or two, then she's off again! I used to push her away as I wanted her to go out and be all independent, but now I realise she just needs me to be there briefly, and show her I have confidence in her to go off again."

Kim:
Tell me about the various clients who seek your support?

Robyn:
The program is designed for caregivers of children who are four months of age through to 6 years old. Since COVID-19, and using Zoom as the platform, I have had a broader range of people benefit: young parents, carers of babies, through to primary aged children and even a few adult children as well as grandparents! I've had foster carers and adults who have no children of their own, but have nieces and nephews, or work with children.

Kim:
The Circle of Security has a registered graphic (which Chris Munro has artistically recreated with his own style on page 111) that suggests this approach is only for infants and young children, which is perhaps a bit of a myth?

Robyn:
Yes, it's relevant for all of us, no matter our age. There are four basic needs on the circle for when the child goes out in the world to explore, and then there's four needs on the circle when they come back into their safe haven.

Kim:
What are these basic needs?

Robyn:
The four "going out" needs are: Watch Over Me, Delight in Me, Help Me and Enjoy with Me. The four "coming in" needs are: Protect Me, Comfort Me, Delight in Me and Organise My Feelings.

"Delighting in" is on both sides of the circle because this is the most important need. Being present, in the moment allows for this "delighting in" and is gold for babies – and for all of us.

Kim:
This could even be helpful in supervision with counselling students on placements? This also makes sense for why a grandparent, who simply sits with and follows a young child's every move with a smile, can soon become a special person to the child.

Robyn:
Absolutely. Being with our children is saying "what you are doing is worthwhile and important." This has a positive impact on self-worth and self-esteem. In the "Help Me" need, we can sometimes step in too soon and the child may miss an opportunity to do it themselves, and miss the experience and excitement of achievement.

Last Friday, I picked up my grandson from school and we went to the adventure playground. I got chatting with a parent while watching her son as he climbed on some rocks. He was standing quite high on the rock.

The look on his face was absolute joy and he did a victory pose! Imagine if the parent had intervened to help. There would not have been the same joyous outcome. My grandson then wanted to jump off. We were all transformed from strangers to buddies in a moment of shared delight.

Kim:
And what I'm thinking as you're telling that really poignant story, is some parents might not value independence. Perhaps the child is a girl, and culturally or from fear, this doesn't feel like a good, safe activity to the caregiver? Or they identify with a programmed role as a parent who needs to be protective, so the parent prioritises their wishes over the child's need to explore?

Robyn:
Yes. And because of their own childhood, they may feel compelled to be protective to the degree that the opportunity of connecting with the child's need is lost.

These are called "miscues" in this Circle of Security framework, and the program offers us a new way of identifying when we miscue, and ways to get back on the Circle and meet our child's needs.

Kim:
I love it! We used the Circle of Security in the Mother and Baby Unit, and later when I worked closely with the maternal child and health nurses at the City of Melbourne Family Services Team years ago. You're refreshing my memories and I can see this tool may have a more broad application. It could be helpful with parents of teenagers. It makes me wonder if a lot of the current problems with teenage motivation to do chores or homework around extrinsic/intrinsic motivation could stem from these early days?

Are some adolescents perhaps now waiting for external help or prompts? Maybe they are not used to having a go on their own, messing up, and having another go, and then celebrating successes. If we train children to wait for our cue to take action, or we step in and take over when they are little, initiative may not develop? Then in the teen years, when it's that time of night when they're supposed to go and do their homework, they may be almost dependent or addicted to the external voice, the extrinsic motivation, even if it looks like they are being nagged. Yet developmentally they will be rebuffing being controlled!

Maybe children lose connection to themselves if our critical or controlling voice is too big?

This parenting work is so vital to the foundation of all children's relationships with themselves and others, and stepping towards their own adulthood responsibilities.

Robyn:
Yes, and there are a couple of books by Pennie Brownlee that speak to this area of cultivating intrinsic motivation at an early age. *Magic Places* introduces ideas about the beginnings of drawing for children, the importance of the scribbling stage and encouraging parents to show delight in the marks their child is creating on the page. The

other book, *Dance With Me in the Heart*, is an adult's guide to great infant-parent partnerships. Both are wonderful books.

Kim:
So, meeting the child where they're at, without imposition of our ideas? Avoiding saying, "Why don't you try and draw a house like your big brother?"

Robyn:
Yes, it brings me back to when I was at school in the art room, and I felt scared about what I was going to create out of this lump of clay in front of me! I want all children to feel free to create!

Kim:
We often come to know what is important because of our own, early wounds. What other topics are covered in the course?

Robyn:
The Circle of Security is an eight-week program for parents. The first week the basic circle is presented as a card game and gives a novel insight into this circle of going out, and coming in. In week two, the needs are demonstrated through watching video examples, and a guessing game of the needs that children show through their behaviours.

Weeks three and four cover a central topic of what it means to be present and "be with" our children on the circle. We explore six core feelings and attention is paid to our own experiences of being parented. We explore the shift from "knowing," to resting in "being" and we watch video examples of "being with" our child.

Weeks five and six explore our struggles on the Circle, and again the video examples demonstrate a "no blame" approach, whilst shining a light on our automatic parenting styles and opening up new possibilities to make new choices. The good news is it is never too late to get back on the Circle, no matter the age of your child.

Kim:
Can you give an example of what the parent may experience when they put these ideas into practice?

Robyn:
Sure. For a parent who felt that expressing anger was not ok when they were a child, it may be a struggle for that parent to connect and be with their child, and understand how they can respond when their own child expresses anger.

The program helps parents to reflect on their natural reactions and to choose a different response that is going to result in a closer connection with their child.

Last week, in our Zoom group, one parent shared, "Every single time I remained calm, it always worked with my five-year-old child. Just the other day after a few tears, she just wanted to be held and rocked. She was still upset as she wasn't able to have what she wanted, but I was able to be with her. I am starting to say little things like 'does your loving cup need filling up?' and 'it looks like you have some worries,' instead of using the word 'anxieties' and 'you can tell me about any worries.' I can still keep firm and reasonable boundaries."

Kim:
This sounds like parents can discover a new attitude, and accept that "this is what's happening" for their child right now. It sounds like the parents feel safe in this group environment. They can see that others also struggle, and that emotions come and go: sadness, anger and frustration, and that what is needed is acceptance.

Robyn:
I acknowledge all the parents for being so courageous in sharing their struggles.

Kim:
Last century parenting practices included smacking, ignoring, exclusion and expulsion to your room, and timeout, which is all about disconnection. Now parents are told to practice time in. Parents are being asked to sit with a dysregulated child and not exclude them, and all this is so new.

Robyn:
Yes, "sitting with" and pausing is gold for our babies and children. I have another example from a parent who shared, "My son wanted grapes the other day when I didn't have any, and at first I found it hard to 'be with' him in his disappointment. I repeatedly told him 'I don't have grapes,' and was cross at him when he threw the strawberries I'd offered across the room." The mother said she thought about how to be his secure base and found a way to acknowledge his feelings. She said, "Ah, you wanted grapes," in such a way that the child felt understood. Then they explored other fruits that he could choose, or he could choose not to eat.

In the program we explore how human beings thrive on acknowledgment, together with the "pause" moment, so these ideas were put into action to assist the toddler's brain adjust to the fact there were no grapes.

> "Keep working on you.
> Remind yourself that it's your emotions and experiences and expectations that are causing your outbursts, not your little one's behaviour."
>
> — L.R. KNOST

Kim:
And knowing that he was heard, and he did not feel shamed. These so-called meltdowns can then become opportunities for relationship repair and connection?

Robyn:
Yes, and the connection created a calm space between the parent and child, for the child to have the capacity to think, and make a new choice between what fruit was actually available.

Cause and effect can be reactive and destructive, or powerful and connecting! Janet Landsbury, an American Educator writes:

> "In my world there are not bad kids.
> Just impressionable, conflicted young people
> wrestling with emotions and impulses,
> trying to communicate their feelings and needs
> the only way they know how."

When we can pause and bring our "kind and firm" adult rational mind into the relationship we can create smooth sailing, and children learn they can't have everything they want in life in a way that is supportive and not shaming.

In weeks five and six, we talk about the empathic shift from "reacting with our feelings towards our child's behaviour" to "responding with our behaviour towards our child's feelings."

Kim:
Parents might see their child go towards the rubbish bin, and their fear of their child getting germs, sick or dirty causes a big reaction. But a child can't understand what the parent's loud voice is about.

Robyn:
Yes, parental fears get in the way. It is in these moments that the course does its best work.

Week six shares video examples of how "Bigger and Stronger" can turn into "mean" and how "Kinder and Wiser" into "weak."

> "Remember, no matter the problem, kindness is always the right response.
> When your child is having a problem,
> stop, listen, then respond to the need, not the behaviour. The behaviour can be addressed later, after the need has been met,
> because only then is the door to effective communication truly open."
>
> — L.R. KNOST

Kim:
And is it ok that the children sometimes experience the parent being mean or weak? Because parents are growing and learning too. This is what it's all about, being ok with mistakes. But parents often really want to get it right.

Robyn:
Yes, and I often say, "We are not made to be perfect!"

Kim:
With new clients I ask, "What are your intentions for coming to family counselling?" They often say with a straight face, "Oh, we

want to be a happy family." And so I will say, "Are you talking about a 100% happy family? Or would you be ok with 80% or 60%?' And that kind of blows people over a bit because they actually can see that it's a false hope to live even one whole day with your children, where everyone's performing at 100%.

Robyn:
Beautiful. That leads us to the seventh session, which is about repair. The video examples focus on how we can repair the ruptures in our relationships with our children. We build deeper connections, take responsibility and make new agreements with each other – time and time again.

Repairing relationships with a "time in" approach is the basis of secure attachments. The final week eight is a summary and there is a very poignant before and after video of a parent and child where you see the shift from rupture towards repair, and a special reconnection in their relationship.

Kim:
I like to use the metaphor of a broken bone in the body. Once a bone is broken and it starts to knit, it's stronger than the original bone. And I think that metaphor is very helpful to allow parents to let go of some of this guilt and shame about their previous ways of interacting.

It is a principle I use in couples therapy too. Arguments happen; it matters more what you choose to do next. When partners learn how to repair ruptures, and have learnt to talk to one another, listen to one another, well they feel a stronger bond, right?

Robyn:
That is a very useful metaphor, thank you!

A key part of the program is supporting parents towards an empathic shift, and creating a new view that their child is saying, "I need you, but I don't know what to do with what I am feeling." Parents learn to practise "the pause" and return to the Circle with kind and firm hands.

Kim:
I was working with a parent the other night who had sought counselling after the breakdown in her relationship with her 15-year-old daughter. It was our sixth and last Employee Assistance Program (EAP) session. She reported that she had decided to prioritise the connection with her daughter, over saying "yes" and doing the usual, extra hours of overtime at work.

As a single mum, now her daughter was older, she'd been prioritising work. Through counselling, she chose to make time for repairing the rupture in her relationship by being open about her previous misguided priority of work. She had even asked her daughter what kind of relationship she wanted? Very impactful.

This kind of work, supporting parents who are ready to take responsibility to improve their relationships, means we may not even need to see the child.

Robyn:
That's a lovely story of this review and reconnection process. When I first completed the Circle of Security training, I went home and started repairing lots of aspects of my relationship with my daughter. It's never too late to build secure relationships with our child, even with adult children! It is just like that metaphor of the broken bone: when using these tools, the relationships only get stronger.

Kim:
Bringing this all together, Robyn, you have also used the Circle of Security to help you see old patterns, then you made a decision to do some reflective work, and find opportunities to implement these ideas with your adult daughter.

Robyn:
Adults can have strong emotional responses from the past, and this can be confusing for our children. Making that adult decision to take personal responsibility to repair and find new ways of responding

builds healthy relationships with our children going into the future. Self-compassion and compassion for our children is key.

Kim:
I have loved hearing about your areas of expertise, and your passion. What's it been like for you having this conversation today?

Robyn
Oh, it's been really great Kim, and thank you for this opportunity. Sharing with you reminds me of why I do this work.

Bio:

Robyn works within her local community and organisations as an Infant Mental Health Practitioner and facilitates the Circle of Security programs privately. Robyn loves sharing 'aha' moments, shifts in perspectives and new ways of being as she helps people connect more deeply with their partners, friends, family and children.

Email: robyn@supportnet.com.au
Website: https://www.selfworthbeyondbirth.com

Qualifications:
Registered Circle of Security Parenting Educator; Post Grad in Infant and Parent Mental Health; Certified in Infant Massage and Newborn Assessment tool; B.Ed.

CHAPTER 8

Releasing Hidden Creativity as an Aid to Therapy

with Dalit Bar

Kim:
Welcome to our interview, Dalit. Could you or your family have predicted, when you were a little child, that you'd become an art therapist?

Dalit:
First of all, thank you Kim for inviting me to participate. The fact is, I never would have predicted that I would become an art therapist! Certainly, I've always loved art, ever since I remember myself as a young child.

After I finished high school, I trained and worked as a graphic designer for about 20 years before I made the transition into studying counselling and art therapy. What I can say however, is that art has always had a calming effect on me: it was my safe place, a place to which I could escape. So, the transition from graphic design to becoming a full-time therapist has been a long journey.

Kim:
Tell me more about what this graphic design work looked like – 20 years is a long time.

Dalit:
I had some years creating greeting cards, and really enjoyed doing the illustrations, but I also enjoyed layout design and typography projects. There was a lot of variety. Then I began to feel a need for something deeper, and searched for more of a connection with the work on a psychological level. I began reading and questioning, and seeking a better understanding of my own thoughts and emotions as expressed in my creativity.

I studied creative therapies and counselling for many years, and I loved it. And I love what I do now. Art therapy is my passion. It's funny for me to think about the fact that now I run my own private practice!

Kim:
And so here you are! And how fortunate are we that you'll be facilitating an art therapy workshop at my next supervision retreat!

Dalit:
It's wonderful, yes, and very interesting how life can take you in different directions.

Kim:
And how did you first begin that journey into the therapeutic side of art?

RELEASING HIDDEN CREATIVITY AS AN AID TO THERAPY

Dalit:
The first memory that comes to my mind is a memory of myself as a teenager, painting a self-portrait. Back then I had migrated to Australia with my family and I was homesick. I struggled being in my new adopted country. Painting a self-portrait was difficult but it helped me realise the depth of my sad feelings and reflect on them.

Later on, when I was in my mid-30s, I was again searching for a deeper understanding and meaning around my life circumstances. I discovered that making art proved to be a good outlet and helped me to deal with my challenges.

Along with immersing myself in creativity, I started reading about art as therapy and considered studying it. I was also inspired by a friend who took part in an art therapy group for cancer survivors. She found the process very helpful and healing, and I decided to study it professionally. I wanted to give it a go. My first course was a Graduate Diploma in Experiential Creative Therapies. I then studied a bachelor's degree in counselling followed by a Master of Art Therapy.

Kim:
I'm thinking, but I might be wrong, that 20 years ago art therapy was even less well known and understood. Were people around you saying, "What? You want to make a career out of this?"

Dalit:
Yes, when I first started studying art therapy I didn't think of it as a career option. I always thought I would continue to work as a graphic designer, as that would enable me to support my family. I worked as a volunteer in hospitals, and community centres doing art therapy. I witnessed how people relate to each other in groups, and how much they got out of the art therapy group practice. Sharing similar experiences and witnessing people's challenges was inspiring to me, especially as I observed the healing benefits of the process.

Kim:
I'm curious, and because I'm not an art therapist, I'm trying to picture you 20 years ago learning about art therapy. Was there a particular painting method, or technique you were drawn to? Was there something that stands out that really drew you in?

Dalit:
The thing that stands out for me the most in the art therapy process is the opportunity for reflection: it's the "gaps" in the process. I really like the reflection; having the opportunity to take the time and stop, and sit there, and see what's going on for yourself.

I always found talk therapy too fast, with not enough time to digest what emerges. However, it has not always been easy. Since I have a visual arts background, I had high expectations of myself to create beautiful work. In the art therapy process, I had to remind myself, it's not about making a beautiful picture; it's about what is going on for me in the moment, and how I relate to that experience through colour, shape and shade.

The second thing that comes to my mind is a case example of a particular client's experience with soft pastels. This client was physically ill, with a motor neuron disease, and mentally struggled with depression. She came to an art therapy group and used soft pastels for the first time. She covered the page with many colours and then smoothed it with her hands. The circular movements of her hands, combined with the colours, created an emotional experience which shifted something inside her. She burst out crying. However, she was grateful for the experience and felt heard and supported by the group. I still think about her often.

Kim:
I can feel her release just listening to you share that story. That is a beautiful and emotive description of the power of art therapy, and about your own struggles with expectations to create a "work of art." And that wouldn't have happened within a couple of months. That would have been quite a journey in itself.

Dalit:
It is a journey, and this is something that I always say again and again to all my clients. It's about reflection and about a willingness to incorporate a new way of thinking. So, I think we always have to remind ourselves that art therapy is not about beauty or aesthetics, or skill, because many people think they have to achieve a degree of "perfection" in what they do or create. So many people announce, "I wasn't any good at art at school," and that sense of failure sticks with them. This is something that continues to be an issue for a lot of people, and sometimes even for myself still. I have to remind clients, don't worry about how it looks, just create and get in touch with the experience.

Kim:
And listening today, that 'reflection time' stands out for me. Was that prioritised in the training? I do think that's missing in a lot of the regular counselling training today.

Can you share an experience about the way you work, and how insight and healing emerges?

Dalit:
I believe the answers are in the process: the process of tuning in to yourself, noticing and reflecting. It is about giving yourself the time to stop and listen. When we are creating, we give ourselves the gift of being in the moment with our creation. In art therapy, the client is invited to continue to reflect on the artwork created, to look at it and to see if anything else comes up.

So, it's a double win, because firstly you get this special time with yourself when you tune in to yourself, sit with what you have made and see what's there. Then you have another opportunity to reflect on it with a trained therapist.

Kim:
So, what does the therapy space look like when a client arrives?

Dalit:
A client comes into the studio and I explain a little bit about art therapy, especially pointing out that art therapy is not about creating beautiful pictures, but that it's about tuning into yourself and expressing yourself in a creative way. I continue to explain that there is no right or wrong, no judgement, that whatever is created in the studio is fine. I emphasise that the therapy is not one-size-fits-all, and that the type of therapy has to suit the person.

The structure of ongoing sessions begins when I greet the client and check in with how they are going, followed by about ten minutes of meditation. I think it is helpful to relax and just to get in touch with yourself before the art-making. Most clients are happy to give it a go.

After the meditation, we move to the table where I have placed a number of different art materials. I work using a non-directive method, so people are free to use whatever art materials they like. I don't introduce too many art materials, as that can overwhelm people who are not used to doing a lot of art. I then support the client to reflect on how are they feeling.

Once the client says that they have finished their art-making, I ask if they're comfortable to reflect on what they have created and then we would have time for that conversation.

Kim:
I'm interested in this reflection time because the research shows we need to be more tuned into the body, and bringing somatic awareness into our therapeutic practice. So, we help clients to develop a felt sense of the energies in their body. Maybe some words will come from that, but it's being with the body that is central to this way of working, and in art therapy, I'm hearing that time is made for exactly this.

Dalit:
Engaging in art-making in a mindful art therapy environment, which is what I foster, helps the client connect the artwork to the body. After the meditation, we explore what sensations are emerging for the client, and where do they feel it in their body. What sort of feelings do they have in their body? Is there some tension?

Depending on the individual's response I may suggest making an image that reflects their experience. A stick figure is fine, for example, just to show where they are feeling different things in their body, and to think about the colours as well, and how different colours represent different feelings. So, then there is a connection to the body.

I have to say that this is not an easy activity for everyone. And especially for the people who have experienced trauma, there's a lot of disconnection from the body. So, this is something that we sometimes have to work on for a while.

Kim:
I'm really so curious about your work and the ways you engage with your clients, finding the language and techniques to use.

Dalit:
I encourage clients to do grounding and breathing exercises. There's one in which you put one hand on your heart and one on your forehead. You sit there quietly and just feel what is going on in the space between the two hands. So, I support clients to connect in that way. As for myself, I meditate most mornings to set the tone for my day, and I write in my journal at night time.

Kim:
Wonderful. I'm so glad we're having this conversation. Where do you get your therapeutic ideas and inspirations from?

Dalit:
I find Peter Levine and Bessel van der Kolk's work very inspiring and helpful in my work.

Kim:
They are both certainly at the top of many practitioners' reading lists. Because it takes a lot of energy doing the work we do with our clients, we must learn to make time for the recovery and recuperation of our precious energies. This may include stimulating our own curiosity about what else is happening out there in our field, attending workshops and so on. You know, there can be a lot of pressure to keep abreast of research and how to implement new ideas. How do you put things in place that help you avoid burnout?

Dalit:
I'm finding at the moment that I'm getting to a place where I need a bit of time out. I feel like I've got to a point where I need a bit of a break. The lockdown, COVID-19 and everything around us, has had an effect too. So, yes, I'm considering taking a break. Also, for me, it's about taking time for my own creativity, and needing time to do my own art.

Kim:
And part of our self-care that we have spoken about before is that pressure when there is some expectation from yourself, and the client.

Perhaps a person is very keen, and we may find it hard to say, "no, I can't fit you in," you know? Part of our self-care is learning to say, no. Just to be able to say "no" takes a while, doesn't it?

Dalit:
Yes, it does actually. For example, this week I got an email enquiry for a client whose needs are not really in my area of expertise. So, I referred them to an organisation that I thought would be a better fit for them, you know, working more with a clinical team, not a single practitioner. It was my opinion that there were severe mental health issues, and the person would benefit from having a team of specialists working together with a range of skills behind them. So, knowing when to say "no," for my own wellbeing and for the benefit of my clients, is an important consideration.

Kim:
And you have to learn that by experience, by taking someone on who at first may not disclose certain problems, and then after a couple of sessions finding this is beyond your area of competence, or feeling it's too intense being so isolated and a sole practitioner when a client has such complex needs.

Dalit:
Yes, that is my feeling too.

Kim:
I wanted to ask about your sources of inspiration. You were at MIECAT, the Melbourne Institute of Experiential Therapies, and other places during your training, and I wondered if there was a particular lecturer or practitioner who really inspired you?

Dalit:
One person in particular was Dr. Warren Lett, who was the founder of MIECAT, he opened my eyes to the value of witnessing a person's creative journey without any judgement. He says in his book, *How the Arts Make a Difference in Therapy*:

> "The success of a session
> is not determined by the number of modalities used or the order of their use
> but rather by the communication
> between therapist and patient during the creative process."
>
> **WARREN R. LETT**

Fifteen years later and having seen numerous clients I can now see even more the merit in his teaching.

Kim:
Your second career is such a contrast to the performance required being a graphic designer where you make something for a purpose.

Dalit:
Yes, it was a big difference for me, transitioning from graphic art to art therapy. A different way of being in the world. This affected my whole life, not just my work. I believe witnessing people's challenges and accompanying them on their healing journey makes me humbler, more grateful and always striving to live by my core values.

I didn't think that I could make a living from art therapy, so that realisation has been very satisfying. I acted on what I was passionate about, and things fell into place. I came across a quote by Steve Jobs which resonates with my experience:

> "The only way to do great work is to love what you do.
> If you haven't found it yet, keep looking. Don't settle.
> As with all matters of the heart, you'll know when you find it."

Kim:

And you wake up in the morning knowing your work aligns with your values, and what you're doing is your passion.

Dalit:

Yes, I am very passionate about the work. I think I live and breathe it.

Kim:

Thanks for your pearls, Dalit. Maybe we can close for today, and later you could add a case example?

Dalit:

Yes, definitely, thank you. I would like to finish by sharing a quote by Shaun McNiff because it reflects exactly my approach to my work:

> "If we can liberate the creative process in our lives,
> it will always find the way to whatever needs attention and transformation."

Case Study

Claire* is a 55-year-old woman who separated from her husband of 20 years. Throughout her marriage, she experienced trauma and had been diagnosed with PTSD. We worked together for about a year using Mindful Art Therapy. We used many grounding, mindful meditations, but in the session I am about to describe, we did the 'leaves on a stream' meditation, which invites the client to notice their thoughts and then gently place each thought on a leaf and let it go - downstream, so to speak. The idea is that we are noticing the thoughts, not trying to get rid of them. Following the meditation, I invited Claire to reflect creatively on some of the thoughts she had while she was in the meditation.

Claire reflected on her frustration with her lack of sleep; she got the oil pastels and started drawing. She then took water colours and added them to her drawing. I invited Claire to look at her drawing and say what she can see in it. She asked herself, "What is stopping me from looking after myself?" She answered: "Avoidance, distractions." Those two words, that she introduced, led the approach to a subsequent deep discussion.

Claire continued to make a second drawing to reflect on the first one. In this drawing, Claire reached out to the oil pastels again, and made strong lines going in a few directions. She wrote the words, "depression, feeling low, sadness, jagged thoughts." This exercise helped her to see that her depression is being fuelled by her avoidance.

After this exercise I invited Claire to focus once more on her thoughts and to see what she needs now.

She drew herself as the lotus flower. Claire reflected on the use of the lotus flower as a metaphor. *"The lotus flower manages to grow out of the muddy water and to become a beautiful flower."* This was a hopeful sign for Claire about the future; that even when sometimes she cannot see through the muddy water, there is still hope.

The following week Claire said she was feeling better with herself, and she could see a shift in her awareness.

She managed to stop and notice her thoughts much more than in the past. She started going to bed earlier and following a healthy sleep routine.

Claire later said that the mindful art therapy had been an amazing journey for her, saying "The process of combining mindful meditation, breathing exercises, creative visualisation, art making, and deep reflection has been a healing progression."

My client gave permission to share this story and the name has been changed to respect privacy

Bio:

In addition to being a mother and an artist, I have over 15 years' experience of working as a counsellor and art therapist in public and private practice in Melbourne. I have a passion for working with children and their families. My aim is to create a healing space where I can support clients to explore and understand the experiences and events that are troubling them.

Website: www.mindsightcounselling.com.au

Qualifications:
Dalit is a registered clinical counsellor.

Master of Art Therapy; Bachelor of Applied Social Science (Counselling); Graduate Diploma in Creative Arts Therapies.

CHAPTER 9

More Than Just a Counsellor
with Nothara Suraweera

"The identity crisis... occurs in that period of the life cycle
when each youth must forge for himself some central
perspective and direction,
some working unity,
out of the effective remnants of his childhood
and the hopes of his anticipated adulthood."
— ERIK ERIKSON

Kim:
Welcome. Nothara, we've known each other for over three years and you're now working in a regional secondary college. I'm wondering if you imagined yourself working in such a role when you were younger?

Nothara:
I never had a clear picture of what I wanted to do when I was in high school. I loved maths and was really good at it, but I didn't really want a career in it. At one point I even wanted to be a chef, but that was short lived. I was always a little unsure of which path I would go down. I've taken life as it comes and followed what has felt right in the moment. I am sure that this role is where I am supposed to be right now in my life.

> "If you can see your path laid out in front of you step by step, you know it's not your path.
> Your own path you make with every step you take.
> That's why it's your path."
>
> — JOSEPH CAMPBELL

Kim:
Were your family and friends surprised when you chose this master's degree in counselling? Were your strengths already shining through?

Nothara:
They all agreed that I've been a 'good listener' and 'understanding,' which I think are kind of prerequisites for a counsellor. My family and my friends can't imagine me in another role now.

> "Hearing is mostly a passive, biological act.
> The way your brain makes sense of sound waves smashing into your eardrums.
> Listening, on the other hand, is not really something you do with your ears,
> but something you do with your soul.
> It is an active decision, hence the term 'active listening.'
> It is a choice, a skill and something that you get better at with practise."
>
> — STEPHANIE JAROSOVA

Kim:
And is there anyone else in this kind of field?

Nothara:
My dad was an accountant and didn't find much purpose in his career; now he works on a farm. His family are teachers and principals, whereas my mum's family line is of holistic doctors and my mum's dad was a chef.

Kim:
There's certainly some nurturing roles there: school principal, teachers, farming, holistic medicine, chefs! So, tell me how you became interested in psychology. When did you start to think about these things?

Nothara:
In high school, I was always really interested and curious in the 'why' behind people's actions, as well as why I might've been experiencing things and responding in a certain type of way. That got me wanting to learn more about how the brain works. I can remember my experience of high school, and how difficult that was personally. Being the eldest of five children in a migrant family also came with many challenges. On top of this, I was manoeuvring through the complexities of puberty while managing a difficult home life with all the cultural differences and expectations.

It seemed normal then, but looking back these things had a significant impact on my wellbeing and mental health. I guess I was developing empathy for others, and understanding that people have internal battles that they may not share. So, in a way I wanted to be a helper in other people's lives, sit with them in their problems and truly understand their pain.

I decided to do a Bachelor of Arts with a major in psychology and criminology. I did some philosophy subjects that I really enjoyed as well, but psych was where my interest lay.

Kim:
And so, you graduated and then what happened?

Nothara:
Once I graduated, I ended up taking a gap year, because I felt that it was a good time for a break. My family had just gone back to Sri Lanka for a year, and I decided to work full-time. I also wanted time to determine whether I wanted to do an Honours in psych or something else.

Kim:
It sounds like you created a space to go up the mountain to reflect on what you wanted to do with your life?

Nothara:
Having that space from my big family and overprotective parents was so needed. I had a year of adventure, and heartbreak, which provided space for reflection and self-discovery. Toward the end of that year, while working through my own difficulties, I really connected with something larger than myself. I became aware of my soul. This was what really began my journey into this counselling role. Like you said, it was very much a going up onto the mountain to reflect.

Kim:
While you studied at Monash where we met, what kind of jobs did you do to make ends meet as a student?

Nothara:
I worked in hospitality. I worked in a café as a barista supervising my own team of staff. I really enjoyed the customer service aspect of working, being able to converse and get to know all kinds of different people and personalities. Before that, I used to be quite reserved and shy, but working in hospitality really helped me to come out of my shell and let go of my own fears of being judged, and to embrace myself.

Kim:
Nothing's ever wasted, is it? And in retrospect, if you hadn't had a couple of years in hospitality, you might not have been that wonderful communicative, engaging counsellor that you are now.

Nothara:
Yes, I totally agree. Every experience has developed me and strengthened the qualities that make me the counsellor I am today. And I'm always changing and growing.

Kim:
Oh, that's so exciting. I love these interviews! So, when you were doing the master's, you studied the units on children and adolescents, couples, CBT and ethics. Was there some point where you thought, "Oh, I really like this?"

Nothara:
I really enjoyed the CBT unit. The tutor made the content relatable and easy to understand. I was also experiencing a personal challenge at the time, and it helped me get insight into my own unhelpful patterns of thinking. I think using what I was learning in my own life consolidated my knowledge.

Kim:
And you know, just as you're talking about your CBT tutor, you've got this lovely warm smile. I'm thinking these connections in life can give us some dopamine. These neuro-transmitters might fire up when we are around someone who fires up our passion.

This reminds me of doing my very first master's, there was this wonderful, warm and wise older woman, Michelle Morris. Probably the age I am now! And she was teaching us grief and loss and she said, "If you don't see grief and loss in a session, you've missed it, because it's in every session." And I remember thinking, "Right. Ok. That's important." And even now, I see loss issues and the need to make space to grieve the losses as part of so many client's stories. I still think of her with such gratitude.

Nothara:
Having tutors that are engaging with their content just makes you want to come to class. It helps you focus and create those connections in your brain, strengthening your memory as well. I can't remember much of what I learnt at uni, but hers was a class that I can remember still.

Kim:
This reminds me of how the safe, therapeutic, relational alliance works with our clients. We watch as they begin to develop that warm spark of joy and interest in their fascinating, unfolding therapeutic journey. After trauma, such moments of self-compassion and secure attachments can create the ground for significant healing.

Nothara:
It's like that quote:

> "I've learnt that people will forget what you said, people will forget what you did, but people will never forget how you made them feel."
> — MAYA ANGELOU

It's the connection that can have the greatest impact. At the end of the day, we're all humans and we were created for connection.

Kim:
Now we are both smiling! What was your master's placement like for you? Was it good preparation for your current role?

Nothara:
Placement was a big part of my master's course and I loved it. I was in a large high school with a really well-structured wellbeing team. Each member of their team was available for support, supervision and I always had the coordinator sign off on my notes. It prepped me well.

Kim:
You mentioned how the welfare team was really well set up. So, if you fast-forward to where you are now, in a small regional secondary college without such a big, all-embracing team, did you initially think: "Oh! Now it's just me?"

Nothara:
Yes! I was like, "oh my gosh" for a while, until I found my feet and settled in. It was challenging being the only counsellor at the school. I worked a lot with the principal, and had regular supervision. I was so grateful, thank you, Kim, for being so accessible and allowing me to double check and ask questions where I was unsure. There wasn't a handover from the previous wellbeing person, and the school had a bit of a gap between that person and myself. This meant I hit the ground running.

Kim:
I enjoyed walking alongside you, learning so much about life in a regional high school, which I now pass on to others! So, what has helped you develop to become this well-regarded counsellor in your school?

Nothara:
As I made that transition, I was able to take on what I learnt at placement. A lot of the weighty stuff included managing disclosures and risks in a school setting – including self-harm, suicidal ideation, sexual assault, family violence and other mandatory reporting. For the safety and wellbeing of the child, as well as to ensure the school is protected, I learnt there always needs to be a "handover of risk," whether to a family member, an external service or both.

A lot of the work around a school is early intervention in mental health support. It's important to know when to refer a client on, which doesn't mean that your counselling has to stop, but it does mean further professional support may be needed.

Something else that was helpful was having peer supervision at my placement school and group supervision through Monash with you. I gained insight into different perspectives of counselling, which helped mould me as a counsellor.

Kim:
How have you managed risk, given parents can become a bit disconnected when their child gets to high school?

Nothara:
As you might remember, speaking with parents was something that I felt quite nervous about starting out. My worries were around the right thing to be saying to them. With practise, I now find myself a lot more confident. I've also had some unpleasant interactions with some parents as well. It's all a learning experience. I've been able to manage those risks by knowing the right local services to contact, whether it be police or the Department of Families, Fairness and Housing (DFFH), Child Protection, Headspace or others.

Kim:
At your school, disciplinary matters are handed over to the senior staff, and the welfare matters are handed to you. And there's a clear distinction. But in other schools, the lines can be blurred. Some counsellors are expected to somehow discipline the child, or say to the parent, "Look, it's really important, you get them to school on Monday." It's great that your role and the counselling space is recognised as sacred for something different from that, isn't it?

Nothara:
During the early weeks of COVID-19 and home schooling, those phone calls home did look like "checking in" with their learning as well. Very soon that shifted to checking in with just the wellbeing of the child and how I could support the families. These calls became special opportunities and helped create connections with parents that centred around how to support their child during hard times.

The staff have been amazing in recognising my role as the counsellor within the school. Recently, I've been calling a parent whose child has struggled with school refusal. My phone calls have been collaborative, and we have worked together well to support the child. It's in those conversations with parents that we can reduce shame, help them feel supported and link them in with services that can work outside of the school setting to support the wellbeing of their child.

Kim:
There can be a fear of, and possibly a history of child protection getting involved, or a concern the school may suspend their child, or you may be going to the police with a criminal matter. It may be drug taking, risky behaviours or consent issues around older students having sexual relationships with younger students. I mean, in a way, you've seen it all now. And it's not the kind of thing you can learn in a university class.

Nothara:
For sure! These things have only been learnt through experience, having good mentors and support at my placement school. Being exposed to these types of situations multiple times has built my confidence in liaising with the appropriate people and services and managing similar issues better.

Kim:
What kind of professional development training have you also sought out?

Nothara:
I attended the Suicide Risk Continuum Training by Headspace. That helped me understand self-harm and suicidal ideation better, as well as interacting with parents around those topics. It really helped me understand my duty of care under the department and gave me guidance on how to handle different situations, as well as where and when to refer on.

Another was the training by the PDP, Professional Development People, called Adolescent Culture: Motivating and Engaging Young People.

I have also used the Mental Health Academy, a PD website accessed through the ACA website which provides videos and texts around specific issues, different client presentations and methods of counselling. It has a great search engine and you also receive a certificate once completed.

I also did some PD's around creative ways of counselling, like your Therapeutic Storytelling and Narrative Therapy. I didn't consider narrative therapy during uni until I met you and now it's the centre of my own counselling practice. I couldn't imagine how I would have gone without those narrative therapy techniques.

Kim:
In any first role, there can be some tension around managing the anxieties and fears of "I'm only freshly qualified. Am I getting it right? Do people respect me?" The university can't provide all the skills you're going to need. So, you're out there, and in your time off you're doing this extra training, on top of a full-time role as a high school counsellor. These stresses can kind of reach a crescendo in these first couple of years out of uni.

Nothara:
Yes. Yes. It was very overwhelming at the start. I was thinking, "Oh my gosh, I don't know everything." And seeing all these different PDs and thinking, "I have to do it all." I used to think I had to be perfect in what I was doing, but looking back I can laugh a little, knowing I have learnt so much in a short time, and this career is one of progression. There's no perfect way to do it. I think the counselling role is intricately blended with your personality, your knowledge and the continued growth of both.

School settings bring with them a lot of different roles. I don't just wear a counsellor's hat. My title is wellbeing coordinator, which involves coordinating programs, facilitating workshops and group work, liaising with teachers and staff, and even staff wellbeing.

A lot of my work also involves managing disclosures, mandatory reporting and co-regulating with highly anxious students. A lot of things can just pop up on the day, which has meant I've had to learn how to manage my days and my energy. I think it's very different to just being a counsellor with clients booked in each hour.

Kim:
If you touch base in your own body right now, do you feel that you've settled in, you're more comfortable in your body as the counsellor than in those early months?

Nothara:
Now reflecting on that, and checking in with my body, I am more comfortable, and I trust myself a little more. I can feel a sense of peace in my chest area.

Kim:
Sometimes when you're new to counselling, you're too busy for self-care, and because of the excitement and joy at having a meaningful role, you may think you don't actually really need it. There's a certain invincibility when you begin something new. A rush of energy and passion. All that adrenaline!

But then, the body gets overloaded. Monday to Friday with the stress of a steep learning curve and a huge responsibility. The department says, "Thank you very much, here's your minimum wage." And then as burnout starts to emerge, which happens to everyone at some point in their career, could you share how you coped as that threshold approached?

Nothara:
One of the biggest things that's helped me is cutting back to a nine-day fortnight, which you suggested. I was worried about asking for it, wondering if other staff would judge me or think I was not capable, or even think I can't manage stress. I'm glad I had the courage to ask, in spite of those thoughts. The way I see that decision to ask now is that I was acting proactively and protectively to maintain my wellbeing.

Kim:
And in a regional setting, every single child is known, so all the staff can become almost like proxy family around the young people, which can add an additional stress, but what an amazing opportunity to have this connection. Can you share more about how you support and deliver training for staff?

Nothara:
There was a big focus on staff wellbeing during 2020 and this poured over into the second year of COVID-19. During remote learning I remember doing some talks around the importance of self-care and work boundaries when staff suddenly found their home respite had become their workplace.

I also hold some mindfulness meditation sessions for staff during professional learning days. The first term back was quite challenging for everyone, and towards the end of term, everyone was tense and ready for a break. So, we got together and had a meeting with all staff and shared some good moments, bad moments and some ugly moments that had happened. It was really important to take an intentional break to acknowledge each other and the challenges that had come up, and celebrate together.

Kim:
So important to come together. And what kinds of therapeutic approaches have you found helpful with your young people?

Nothara:
With older students we may analyse things a little bit more, which makes sense too developmentally. I integrate CBT with psychoeducation around thinking styles and patterns, and linking this to emotions and behaviours, which comes up a lot just before exam time.

Kim:
So, teaching about the brain?

Nothara:
Yes, I love psychoeducation around how our brain works, it has so much power. I bring in mindfulness practices, whether it be a two-minute grounding at the end or picking a question out of the "gratitude jar," and answering it together.

Creative counselling works really well with young people, and your first book has been so helpful with that. The "Team of Life," which is strength-based, as well as "The Fork In The Road" technique, where the client may be faced with a choice leading into two different directions have all been great. I have found the use of visuals in session can really advance an understanding of what has been happening inwardly and externally. Oh, and narrative timelines! Probably one of the most used practice in my sessions.

I see the counselling space a little bit like keeping a journal. If you're someone that journals often, you find it becomes a sacred space where you make time to reflect on your day: the things that you're grateful for and the challenges that came up, and how you worked through them. It also helps us recognise times where we may have strayed from our values. In a similar way, the counselling space allows for those reflective questions to be asked that a young person may not have the capacity to ask themselves. It's a space to foster awareness and a heightened sense of who we are.

Kim:
Your counselling room may be the only safe, confidential space for young people to reflect about life. And there's always such a breadth of concerns that young people today struggle with.

Nothara:
There's definitely a lot of depression and anxiety presentations. Loss, low mood, self-harm and thoughts of suicide, negative thoughts, gender questions, changes in eating habits, feelings of anger and troubles with sleep. There's also cyber issues, family violence disclosures and sexual assault disclosures.

Kim:
Even though we're talking about young people growing up in the 21st century, and there should be no stigma around talking about these things, there will be still a portion of young people that are embarrassed or cautious about talking with a counsellor, or anyone! Others might wear their depression as a badge, as I recall fondly from one of our supervision sessions.

Nothara:
Yes, both ends of the continuum. I have found that males can find it particularly difficult to talk about their problems.

With new students I ask if they are ok with me taking them from their class, because everyone can see. Nearly all of them say yes, though a few prefer an appointment slip, so it's more discrete. It's good that the wellbeing team is integrated into the school quite openly, to really reduce that stigma and highlight the importance of seeking support when needed.

> "Remember, seeing a counsellor, social worker, psychologist or therapist for your mental health should be as encouraged and revered as seeing a personal trainer, physiotherapist, exercise physiologist or chiropractor for your physical health. Health is health!"
>
> — LANA-JOY DURIK

Kim:
How do you manage confidentiality around staff? Last century, if a teacher came up to a school welfare person and asked how Johnny is going, there may have been and exchange about Johnny, which we now would classify as inappropriate disclosure. I don't think things were as clear back then around ethics. In talking with parents, we've also really tightened that up. How do you protect that confidentiality?

Nothara:
In a rural school, it can be tricky to manage confidentially with staff. Everyone either knows a lot of that student's life situation, or they may feel that they need to know something in order to support that student. I find that I've been able to maintain my end of confidentiality by not engaging in conversations when things are brought up about the personal life of that student.

The position I take is, I may take in information, but not give any away. If staff ask, I may either tell them about my ethical obligations around confidentiality, or let them know that I'll speak to the student first and check to see if they are comfortable with any particular information being disclosed. One of my go-to responses for parents or staff is often, "If there are any concerns that you need to be aware of, I will be sure to let you know."

Kim:
That's a great phrase! When a teacher's going through training, they teach a lesson, then the bell rings and it's lunchtime and they sit in the staff room and talk openly about the children. So, suddenly a person is in their school, who's *not* telling and *not* sharing what they know about the student. Quite challenging to juggle these issues.

How do you receive your referrals?

Nothara:
The year level co-ordinator gathers input from teachers about concerns and usually makes a phone call home to let the parent know that their child will be getting some wellbeing support or seeing the school counsellor. However, if a student self-refers, that conversation with the parent does not really take place. In a couple of situations, parents have asked me to stop counselling their child.

Kim:
Is that generally a parental fear of other agencies getting involved?

Nothara:
Definitely. I have found that a particular response to the fear of agencies being involved is actually an indicator for the potential for those agencies to become involved, or have been involved, especially with risk or safety issues.

Kim:
So, that child might not get the counselling they need.

Nothara:
Yeah. It's an unfortunate reality, but that does sometimes happen.

Kim:
Can you offer some tips for someone who picks up this book and reads your chapter, who becomes interested in working in a secondary college?

Nothara:
First, I think finding an amazing supervisor for regular support, especially when things come up and you're not sure, is really important. For me, having you as a supervisor was such a big help as you were willing to walk on that journey with me, and provide that support I needed as a frantic new counsellor. You also provided the space to explore those creative ways of counselling which opened my mind up to different ideas.

I highly recommend doing targeted PDs, especially suicide risk training.

Boundaries! The importance of boundaries within the client-therapist relationship. When I started out, ending sessions on time was tough. I felt like I needed to find the "right time" to end sessions, rather than keeping it in within the 40 minutes, and slowing down a few minutes prior to check in how the session was helpful.

Not responding to emails outside of school hours is part of those boundaries. Knowing how to manage your workload, so you are not taking work home is something to be set up early on and then maintained as part of self-care.

At a school, there is also professional contact with clients outside of session. For example, going on school camps, being a part of school events, seeing them in the yard at recess and lunch. The student gets to see a different side of the counsellor. Those interactions can also help you learn more about a student.

Kim:
Thank you so much, Nothara. You have given us an insightful tour of the very broad role of a regional school counsellor.

I can't wait for the book to be in your hands, and your chapter to be out there as a resource for others, with all your rich wisdom. I hope you have enjoyed our conversation today.

Nothara:
Yes, I have, it's been great. Such a lovely chance to reflect on how far I've come.

Bio:

Nothara said, "I love baking desserts and then eating them, sharing a meal with the people I love and having a boogie to some favourite tunes."

Email: nothara.95@gmail.com

Qualifications:
Secondary School Counsellor; BA; M. Couns.

CHAPTER 10

Hearing the Voice of the Child: Working with Parents in the 21st Century

with Kim Billington

Interview by Natasa Denman,
owner and founder of Ultimate 48 Hour Author

Nat:
Good morning Kim. Your first book *A Counsellor's Companion: Creative adventures for child counsellors, parents and teachers* became an Amazon #1 Bestseller!

You reached out to the Ultimate 48 Hour Author team in the Melbourne lockdown of September 2020, saying the cosmic algorithms led you to us! Within six months you had written and published your first book – congratulations.

So, tell me, I'm curious why you chose the title of our conversation today, "Hearing the voice of the child?"

Kim:
Thanks Nat. I often use "the last century" as a kind of metaphor for our thinking. So, last century, people really weren't that interested in hearing the voice of the child. Children were to be seen and not heard, and pretty much silenced and shut down: "No, you've done the wrong thing. Go to your room, no pocket money for a week!" And that's because the adults, the parents or the teachers weren't aware that the child's behaviour is being driven by some strong emotions that may be too big for the child to handle. And if you're a child, what do you do with big feelings? It can end up in a behaviour that doesn't look so good, or it gets swallowed, which can impact self-worth. So adults need to learn to hear what is behind behaviours.

To help their child, parents can learn the language of emotions and, when possible in the present moment, watch their own bodily responses when something upsets them. There can be a slight tension in the chest or belly, it may rise up to the throat. These hidden, inner energies (emotions) are on the move, and counsellors can teach parents to show the child how to locate them by putting their own hand where the emotion is, and pressing lightly. As soon as parents put their hand where that energy is, a deep breath is activated, followed by a sigh, calming the stress response.

When they can do this with their child, we call it co-regulation, which can lead to more relaxing family communications about everyone's wishes, hurts, hope and needs.

To begin, we sit still and notice the presence of a 'felt sense' (a vague fluttering or tightening feeling), and words are not needed. This is called the emotional-somatic feedback loop. Parents can create a welcoming, safe space for these teachable moments. This will help the child regain a normal heart rate after an upset, allow for a conversation about the problem, and help their brain to make better choices next time.

Conversations about discovering the what and where of feelings increase the child's emotional intelligence, and are opportunities for precious connection times. Everyone has these things called feelings!

Nat:
So, creating a safe place to hear the voice of the child is central to the book?

Kim:
Yes, and "hearing the voice of the child" represents the seismic shift from last century ideas about children, to the 21st century. All the neuroscientific research about the child's needs for optimal social brain development shows we've been harming children's mental health by prioritising cognitive development, and focusing on children's negative behaviour as a measure of their identity, and ignoring the development of emotional awareness and social ways to express emotions.

The aim last century was to bring up children who did as they were told, by whatever methods seemed to work: criticism, coercive motivation, punishments and time-out. Longitudinal research shows that these practices resulted in a sense of rejection, failure, shame and anger. Such ongoing parenting practices can disrupt the development of a stable sense of self, and the ability to form healthy, secure adult relationships. Children who regularly experience rapid heart rates when afraid and confused can find it hard as adults to breathe deeply and manage stress.

As a child and family counsellor, I see the parents first, and create a safe space to hear the voice of the parent, where they can reflect on their own behaviours without shame. This is where I can offer some information and coaching around breathwork to help with their own emotional regulation. We can create Emotional Regulation Plans (ERPs), and each family member can have a few things that work for them listed as a menu.

I need to get a history of what life has been like for the parents, and what their hopes are for their family. What direction are they wanting to go? What will it look like? What are they already doing well? What do they admire about their child?

Most parent's default when they are under stress will be a repeat loop of their own parent's intergenerational patterns. What parent hasn't one day thought, "I sound just like my mum/dad!"

I need to be working with parents as they are the ones who see the child every day and can be demonstrating how to be the person they want the child to grow up to become.

> "Don't worry that children never listen to you;
> worry that they are always watching you."
> — ROBERT FULGHUM

These parent "intake" conversations often include eliciting stories of previously unprocessed hurts and traumas from their own childhood.

Their own child's behaviours can often trigger old and frightening intergenerational responses, and a counsellor can help with that. Parents may describe the child as being "angry" or "defiant." At some point, as we are unpacking the history of the label and the problem, parents often notice that the apple hasn't fallen far from the apple tree!

Last century many parents and teachers were not aware or interested in the reasons why a child was experiencing emotions, or how distressing the feelings were for the child. Nobody ever thought to really pause, look, or ask out of genuine curiosity, "Is this a big, middle-sized or a small feeling? Are you ok? What do you need?" Containing and supressing emotions became a 20th century childhood survival skill. That is too toxic to repeat in the 21st century.

In fact, until recently, nobody made space for a child to even ask questions about things like the painful loss of a family separation. I've heard it said that the distress of a divorce is like a bird's nest being torn in two. Chapter 7 in my first book is called "The Unfairness of Loss," which follows a chapter called "The Roller Coaster of Emotions." This new, empathic approach to hearing and understanding children's suffering would not have formed part of a parenting book 50 years ago. Fortunately, this has changed.

A child with strong emotions needs the kinder, wiser adult to show them how to safely reconnect to themselves, and respond to their feelings and find out what's going on.

> "The goal with kids is not to get them to be calm...
> Calm is not the point.
> Connected to self during any and every experience is the point."
>
> — LISA DION

Nat:

Beautiful. So, talk to me about these big and little emotions. I am very curious.

Kim:

Well, Nat, mostly it was never safe when you were little to challenge your own powerful parent who may have abused their power to control you, or used hurtful labels. We rarely could have said, "Please don't do/say that, it makes me scared/sad."

All that hurt never goes away. Decades on, most parents still recall the hurtful names they were called: lazy, selfish, naughty. They can find themselves being triggered by things their own children now say or do. Years of supressed fury and worries may emerge as stress, anxiety and depression.

I use the babushka doll toy as a metaphor to address the parent's earlier childhood struggles. I say, "We present to the world as if we are all grown up. Like the largest, outer babushka doll. But as we look inside, if we unpack it, each doll represents earlier experiences and hurts, and ways we've adapted and learnt to stay safe. At last, we come down to the teeny, tiny one, which is when you were still in your mother's tummy."

Having self-compassionate conversations with our younger self is called re-parenting. Parents can do this to heal their own childhood resentments and attachment hurts. This "self-talk," with hands on belly and heart might look like, "Hello, my little six-year-old self. (Deep breath.) Nobody was there for you when you were scared. (Deep breath.) I'm here for you now. We have survived those times. I hear you and validate you. You did your best. (Deep breath.)"

> "Freedom from fear
> could be said to sum up
> the whole philosophy of human rights."
> — DAG HAMMARSKJOLD

Every child has their own unique emotional ways of responding to life's troubles. Our birth order, temperament, genetics, expectations and family dynamics are all formative in our identity development, which includes how we choose to express ourselves. If you have three children, you know that they may all have the same parents, but whoa, what different children!

Nat:
I love that. So, tell me, where do children feel these emotions?

Kim:
Young children may say they've got a tummy ache, or an older child a headache before school or a night away from home. At that point,

a parent can either pause and see the child with empathy, or react to the child's "inconvenient" behaviour which they may judge as being simply a ruse to get out of doing some chore, or getting their uniform on for school.

Basically, emotions live invisibly inside the body, so I coach the parents how to locate their emotion and teach this to their child: "Put your hand on your own tummy, press a little bit, and take a breath in. Now let it out nice and slowly. Ahhh. Yeah. I feel it. You can ask your child to do the same. Say to them, 'show me where you feel it. What's there? That wobble is a feeling telling you something. What is it saying? Let's take another breath: in through the nose, and out through the mouth. We can talk to the feeling: 'Ooh, hello, little feeling. I am with you. I'll be with you today.'"

The science behind this is clear. Ignoring strong emotions leads to illness. I often share Dr. Gabor Maté's YouTube videos, such as his authenticity vs attachment one. They are short and simple wake-up calls for parents.

Nat:
So, we're teaching them about emotions and how to work through them?

Kim:
Yes, and there's three stages: noticing, being with and choosing a strategy to self-regulate and reduce overwhelming emotions. Of course, if the child has moved from a little bit of frustration up to a furious rage, then in that moment, when they're heightened, you can't even speak to them! They won't hear you. It's the same with us. When we become heightened, we stop listening. So we need to choose to pause, and make time to talk later when things have calmed down.

Parents and children can work together as a team on noticing how and when these feelings arrive, and find what works for the child. These things will need to be repeated regularly, and can't be taught as a one-off practice. It's just like learning a new language. It can help to find an exciting name for any new skill, perhaps we may call it the 'Getting to Know You Project.

> "The capacity for self-soothing is born out of hundreds and hundreds of instances of being soothed by someone else."
> — RACHEL SAMSON

This is quite a big task! Child counselling, for that reason, should really involve other family members so no one child feels like the "problem child."

One hack I ask parents to use to break entrenched patterns of harsh parenting styles or challenging behaviours, is to treat the child as if they were a guest in the house for three days.

Parents speak so politely for a while, and this makes them realise they are often actually quite judgemental, and don't tune in or listen to their child. This hack requires an adult choice, to not confront children when they are heightened emotionally.

We can later address what went wrong and say, "Look, last night at dinner, there was this upset, let's talk about it. Is that ok?" We can offer an apology if we began yelling and frightened the child, and this may help repair the rupture in the relationship. "What do you need me to say next time I see you getting upset? I didn't respond in the best way last night, I'm sorry. How can we manage it better next time?" When we apologise and take responsibility for our own reactivity, the child can model from this too.

Instead of, "Go to your room! This is timeout!" the current guidelines are, if you are calm enough, stay nearby and "be there" for "time in" with your child.

With older children, we may show them a "T" sign with our hands as a symbol that *we* need some space, and say, "I'm going to go and have some time away. I'm going to hang the washing out and take a few deep breaths for a few minutes so I can calm down."

It's very hard to express how you're feeling in words when you're heightened with an emotion, because the brain is in fight/flight/freeze and the brain's survival skills bypass the language part of the brain. I get some families to have a variety of helpful responses already on little pieces of card to hold up when they are too upset to speak nicely! Things like, 'I need a cuddle' or 'I can't talk about it now.'

Nat:
Yeah. I've heard that in the adult world, making decisions when we're emotionally too high or too low is not the right time. We need to wait till we come back to neutral before we can make a more thought-through decision. You can't speak to someone who's going through anger and rage, or is really sad. So that's interesting to know, isn't it? Adults can forget what it was like to be a child.

Kim:
Totally, Nat. And our own childhood memories are never far away. Parents can also be triggered by something that happened to them at a similar age, because as Bessel van der Kolk said, *"the body keeps the score."* The body never forgets your own big and little traumas, you know? So, if you're with a ten-year-old and they're having a flip out, it might be that as a ten-year-old child, you yourself were chastised severely, and shamed whenever you flipped out.

Even reading this, some people may become heightened. How is your heart rate now, recalling some childhood traumas? Often, we have one particular event from our childhood on a repeat loop. Having a big sigh is an excellent stress-release strategy. You can put your hand on your chest, and your other hand on your belly and let out a loud sigh. "Ph-ooo. Hmm. Ok. Yeah, here we go. I'm the adult now. I'm no longer the frightened, angry, powerless child. Those bound-up energies are still there, sending me a message from the distant past." Counselling parents involves helping them process that pain, and this is what re-parenting can do.

When we are in distress, we can't access the frontal cortex, which is the brain's executive tool. This part of the brain does not complete its development until our mid to late 20s. So young children need us to model how to notice emotions before they overwhelm the child's immature brain's capacity to cope.

Nat:
That's amazing, that the body's imprinting stays with us forever. In your first book, you talk about learning to "connect before we correct." You know, parents can be wanting to be in control. So, how do we manage those situations?

Kim:
Once the child knows the parent sees them, hears them and wants to connect, and not to shame or control them, there's a huge shift in the child. They feel safe enough to tell the parent how they feel and what they need, and can tolerate being gently corrected because their connection with the parent is secure.

Parents can choose connection, and practise noticing and responding to their own anger before it gets too big and they flip out. It can also help to use a bit of humour with children.

> "Don't forget to bring your funny bone along
> on your parenting journey.
> Humour is a universal language
> that topples walls, connects hearts
> and opens the door
> to communication and cooperation."
> — L.R. KNOST

When your intention is to connect, you find a way to be respectful, "Oh, ok. I hear you. You don't want to eat this dinner I've made, that's fine. I'll try and not be too offended! I'm not going back to the kitchen to make anything special. If tonight you don't want to eat it, so be it. Maybe you can do the shopping with me on the weekend and we can do some cooking together?" Of course, we can't achieve this 100% of the time.

The aim is to help parents self-regulate, so they can co-regulate with their child, and use their rational mind to find a way forward that is empathic and responsive, rather than reactive. Every parent wants to uphold and be in line with their family values and agreed boundaries. These things will be crucial as your child becomes a teenager, and then an adult and goes on to create healthy relationships.

To do this, parents need to identify their beliefs about what they see as important ingredients for a healthy, happy childhood, and envision exactly what they hope their family dynamics will look like. Grudges about past behaviours can be let go of. Barriers to such growth can be identified by everyone in the family. Children can be involved in supporting new changes and will happily offer their ideas too.

> "The secret of change
> is to focus all of your energy,
> not on fighting the old,
> but on building the new."
> — SOCRATES

Parents are amazed at how quickly family problems get smaller once they themselves make that commitment to change their often unconscious, intergenerational attitudes and patterns. What I've learnt is that when children are brought to counselling, it's very often not actually about the child.

Nat:
You talk about using something called The Solution Book: what is that?

Kim:
Oh, Nat that is such a simple idea. With a $2 exercise book, you may not even need to pay money for counselling!

You know, it's magic. Any child or family member can write a problem in this book. Then, once a week for 20 minutes, as part of the family routine, everyone sits down and opens it. Each time, a new 'chairperson' reads out the date and what is written. Then everyone goes, "Ok, let's look at that problem." With eagerness, ideas start flowing, because children are very good at brainstorming! Amazing people!

This process is known as "Family Meetings," and it's described further in the final chapter of my first book. Here is what I suggest: "Keep The Solution Book somewhere near the kitchen, and anyone can write in it what's annoying them or what's on their mind."

So this $2 book is full of problems, but when it is opened together as a family, out pop the solutions! Now, I call that magic! I suggest putting the date next to solutions, too, because you want to make sure you review anything you've discussed in a month's time. Ideas might well need some tweaking.

People can also write suggestions for a birthday party, a holiday or a project. This really is a simple way to "hear the voice of the child" and make time to have some essential fun and laughter with Jenga, a card game, charades and so on.

Nat:
I love it. We have family meetings, but not quite as regularly as that.

Kim:
Family meetings can also become a time to name and celebrate big and small successes. We are modelling to children how to cooperate, manage conflict and thrive as a team. This works equally well in a classroom.

A family or a school cannot be a democracy where "we're all equal," because clearly the parents or teacher has that final responsibility for young people. So, what this approach does is to guide adults to create a safe, collaborative space to hear the voice of the child, and allows children opportunities to exercise some of their ingenuity, power, influence and responsibility.

Nat:
I mean, we know when more heads come together, we're creating the power of the mastermind, aren't we? And young minds are so agile, they can think in many different directions.

Kim:
Yes, and if you only use the Solution Book when there's a problem, it won't work. The magic, the key, that creates solutions is making it regular, and even if there's no problem to discuss, we may randomly pick a name out of the hat and have everyone say something that they appreciate about that person.

Everything I've talked about today, and my whole focus is finding ways to support families to listen to one another, support each other and stay connected.

Nat:
There's so many golden nuggets throughout your book. Congratulations Kim, I really, really appreciate all your tips this morning. I'm going to go and talk to my family about our Friday nights and get that $2 Solution Book.

Kim:
Thanks so much, Nat for this wonderful opportunity. And thanks to the whole Ultimate 48 Hour Author team who helped me from the conception of the idea, through to publishing my first book, which I hope will be a catalyst for change in the lives of children, and put child counselling on the map.

> "If parenthood came with a GPS
> it would mostly just say... recalculating."
> — UNKNOWN

Bio:

Kim has three gorgeous adult children, Claire, Peter and Charli Rose. Kim is grandma to Sterling and his new little sister, Freyja.

After a few years as an RAAF Air Traffic Controller, and then a teacher, Kim retrained as a counsellor and worked in various agencies with different client groups.

Kim now has a private practice for families and children. She provides supervision to counsellors individually and in groups, supervises Monash University's Master of Counselling students on their placements, as well as teaching in the Child and Adolescent unit in the master's course. Kim has been presenting training seminars to counsellors, social workers and teachers for over 30 years. "Never a dull moment," as her own mother, Wyn Billington would say!

Website: https://www.kimbillington.com.au

CHAPTER 11

Four Cornerstones of Counselling

By Kim Billington

Imagine finding a career that fulfils your wish for existential satisfaction and life purpose!

In response to the many FAQs from my Master of Counselling students at Monash University, I have identified four cornerstones of counselling:

1. **The counselling profession:** What exactly is counselling? How might counselling be helpful? What are the various qualifications?

2. **The counsellor:** How do we prepare to be a counsellor? What are the most important things to know?

3. **The client:** What are clients looking for from counselling?

4. **The ethics:** What is essential when meeting the client for that first session? How will I assess my competence? When will I know to refer? How can I avoid burnout?

1. The Counselling Profession

Counselling is a collaborative, sacred and interpersonal journey. It offers a safe and confidential space with a trained professional who can be present and deeply listen, facilitating the client's expression and mastery of their thoughts, feelings, quandaries, conclusions, values, unmet needs and goals.

As the client's reflective capacity increases, they begin to process their life challenges, heal from trauma, identify the patterns that have become maladaptive, and move towards a more coherent and secure sense of self.

The counselling path ahead is as yet unmade, and over time it will be studded with pain, frustrations and magical moments of sparkling therapy.

> "Good... bad? I'm not here to judge where you're at or where you've been.
> I'm simply here to encourage you in where you would like to go.
> You have the map; I'll shine the light on it so you can better read it.
> And eventually, the sun will rise again in your life
> and you'll no longer need my light to assist you."
> — ALARIC HUTCHINSON, LIVING PEACE

The term "therapy" generally refers to medium to longer term counselling (above ten sessions), where the client is ready and wanting to process traumatic experiences, or understand their family of origin trials and tribulations, to better make sense of their current patterns, problems, beliefs, values and identity.

All the research points to the fact that a therapeutic alliance with the client is a better indicator of successful therapy than any one modality, theory or series of interventions.

> "In my early professional years, I was asking the question:
> How can I treat, or cure, or change this person?
> Now I would phrase the question in this way:
> How can I provide a relationship
> which this person may use for his own personal growth?"
> — CARL ROGERS

Qualifications:
There are three main gateway qualifications into the counselling profession: a diploma, a master's or a psychology degree. Many courses post-COVID-19 have been delivered completely online, with only a placement at an agency or school to complete "client contact" hours.

Diploma in Counselling
A typical Diploma of Counselling will offer a broad, general introduction to counselling, and usually takes between ten months to a year to complete. Some courses may not include actual practical placement hours with clients.

Master's Degree
A master's degree in Counselling, Play Therapy, Art Therapy, Music Therapy and so on usually includes one or two years of study, often built upon an existing degree. They can require from 80-100 hours of client contact during a placement in schools or community settings.

About 25 hours of clinical supervision is required.

Some art and play therapy courses also require students to undertake 50 hours of their own counselling.

Registered Psychologists in Australia require a minimum of six years of education and training in psychology, an accredited undergraduate psychology qualification and a postgraduate degree or internship program before becoming registered with the Psychology Board of Australia (PsyBA). A minimum 500 hours of direct client contact is required, and one hour of supervision for every 17 hours of internship. Registry with the Australian Health Practitioner Regulation Agency (AHPRA) is required in order to use the professional title of psychologist, which authorises them to diagnose mental health disorders, and formulate a treatment plan guided by The Diagnostic and Statistical Manual of Mental Disorders (DSM).

2. The Counsellor

Seasoned counsellors often say they follow their intuitions, which refers to our attunement and gut feelings as we become curious about what happened to, and what is still happening with the client. Whatever their theoretical modality, over time counsellors mostly become eclectic, and skilled in disciplined improvisation. They also talk about finding their own authentic way of being with their clients, and ensuring there are moments of lightness and joy as part of therapy.

So, how do we train for this lofty vocation?

Some essential, basic skills include being able to make suicide and family violence risk assessments and tailored, safe responses, as well as being able to clearly and simply introduce the confidentiality clauses to the client. Assessment goes beyond checking off a risk assessment form. Our curiosity about how things look from the client's perspective can include asking about their hopefulness of things improving.

All counsellors should be trained in the complexities of and ways to respond to family violence. According to the last comprehensive survey by the Australian Bureau of Statistics, the Personal Safety Survey 2016, about one in four women (23%) experienced violence by an intimate partner, and one in 13 men (7.8%).

I recommend Jess Hill's three-part SBS documentary, *See What You Made Me Do*, a landmark series about domestic abuse, as a way to understand the patterned behaviour and abuse of power, the prevalence of technology-assisted abuse and how coercive control works.

Our therapeutic, relational stance is important, and most counsellors adopt Carl Rogers' 1950's suggestions, for therapists to be warm, accepting, authentic and non-judgemental. This was in stark contrast to Freud's earlier psychiatric practices, begun in 1886, where the clinician would sit behind and out of sight from the "patient," seeing their role as "analysing" what was wrong with the person they were "treating."

Another central consideration is understanding that all problems will stimulate a stress response in the client, and people will be doing their best to manage this stress. So we can ask, "How do you manage these stresses?"

As human beings, counsellors will have had numerous challenges and stresses in their own lives too. At times, our own unmet childhood attachment needs and traumas may emerge into the client-centred counselling space. When this happens, to get rid of our own distress, we may become overly invested in the speed or direction of a particular client's progress. We may pour our energy into the fire of righteous anger, or over sympathise about the plight of a vulnerable client.

We call these types of counsellor reactions, countertransference. It is a very real, felt sense in us, and we can often notice these moments as bodily energy movements. The session then becomes fleetingly about us, our story and our own disturbances, which will make it hard to be present with the client and their story.

Countertransference is not something to be afraid of. It's not a "bad" thing. It is information for our own review later, and perfect for our next supervision conversation.

When we have a reaction to a client's story, we can ask ourselves: "Why the hurry/upset/fear/weariness/sadness/tension around this particular client, sharing this particular story?"

Along the way, counsellors learn the art of being ok with sitting still and not knowing. We can learn to breathe through the discomforts that arise in session, allowing sacred pauses without being hungry to "fix" something we have judged "fixable."

What is needed is trust in the client's natural wish to follow a healing path towards self-actualisation, and that nothing is actually "broken." It helps to have a deep confidence that the client is the expert about their life, and that they are the ones that need to be making their own decisions about how they live their life and what works for them. Then, working together, we can collaborate on the therapeutic process.

Unlike a friend who may try to problem solve, dismiss, compare their sufferings, or over-sympathise, our training sets us on a path to being able to fully hear a difficult story without leaning in too far, which can happen with new counsellors.

Initially, counsellors may hold some vague belief that we are the "expert," here to "help" the client, so when a client asks for advice, or for sessions outside normal hours, for example, we may say, "Yes." This may be a conflict avoidant reaction, or a wish to come across as genuinely caring. "Yes" is a three letter word that comes with an alarm bell, which sings out: countertransference! Such boundary lapses can turn up later as miscues, confusing the client and jeopardising the therapeutic alliance, and so become ethical issues.

Staying attuned, present and curious about this person in front of you, with a quiet, powerful compassion for their journey of suffering and strengths is our superpower. So much of counselling is about 'being' rather than 'doing.'

> "In order to empathise with someone's experience, you must be willing to believe them as they see it, and not how you imagine their experience to be."
> — BRENÉ BROWN

In the end, the hard yards must be done by the client. There's an apt saying that, "if you're working harder than the client, then it's not counselling."

Early in the engagement, and preferably at intake, we need to enquire about and assess the client's readiness, capacity and willingness to "do the work."

Along the way, we learn how and when to sensitively prepare each client to be challenged, and how to respectfully check in with our clients about the efficacy of our work together.

Routine end of session questions can include, "How was the experience of counselling today? Have you any feedback for me, or can you tell me what was useful today? Is there anything you might do or see differently after coming today?" We can pull up the whiteboard and write down three things that stood out from the session, and one seed to plant for the next session.

Through an attachment repair lens, the counsellor can be the safe haven for the client. We can model, often non-verbally, what a mindful, respectful and validating relationship might look like. If the client had an insecure childhood attachment, our warmth and responsiveness, or belief that the client can succeed may well trigger protest, despair and detachment responses as they test us to see how genuine we are, or if we are "just another person paid to be kind." This is all normal and ok!

> "...the therapist's role is analogous to that of a mother who provides her child with a secure base from which to explore the world."
> — JOHN BOWLBY

Continual professional learning is also essential. There is an abundance of attachment and neuroscience research, which has led to the development of polyvagal, somatic and movement therapies. We cannot know it all, but we need to be aware of emerging modalities and follow what interests us. A holiday reading list may include: David Wallin,

Susan Johnson, Peter Levine, Stephen Porges, Stanley Rosenberg, Pat Ogden, Janina Fisher, Norman Diogue, Dan Siegel, Daniel Hughes, Allan Schore, Babbette Rothschild, Kristin Neff, Gabor Maté and Bessel van der Kolk to name a few.

Understanding the effects of trauma from a biopsychosocial perspective is central to our work.

> "Trauma is not what bad thing has happened to you,
> but what happens inside you as a result of what happened to you.
> Trauma is an overwhelming threat
> that you don't know how to deal with.
> The first thing that happens in trauma is that you separate from yourself.
> So trauma is disconnection from self.
> Why do we disconnect?
> Because it is too painful to be ourselves."
> — DR. GABOR MATÉ

Our profession requires us to have qualifications, annual registration, clinical supervision and professional development, but these are not worth the paper they are printed on, unless we can focus on developing our compassionate, relational stance.

Miriam-Rose Ungunmerr calls this way of being, Dadirri. Dadirri recognises the deep spring that is inside us, and can be used as a tool to quieten the mind as it teaches about "the quiet stillness and the waiting." The word is from the Ngan'gikurunggurr and Ngen'giwumirri languages of the Aboriginal people of the Daly River region of the Northern Territory.

Henri Nouwen calls such a stance, spiritual hospitality:

> "The beauty of listening is that those who are listened to start feeling accepted, start taking their words more seriously and discovering more about themselves.
> Listening is a form of spiritual hospitality."
>
> — HENRI J.M. NOUWEN

We walk beside the client who, like a tour guide, shares stories about their life journey. As counsellors, we are trained to offer a mirror and find unique ways to help clients see the bigger picture, and to explore their adaptive and maladaptive inner responses and outer reactions to their life experiences, past and present, and clarify their preferred ways of living according to their values, hopes and dreams.

We need to be interested in "The Person" as well as "The Problem," and I have found such a lens from the narrative therapy toolbox helpful to balance this work, so we don't become as stuck as the client in a problem-saturated story.

My own explorations at intake may include drawing six circles on the whiteboard, and asking, "What are the top three troubles in your life at the moment, and the top three easier moments/helpful people/enjoyable activities?" When a client discloses feelings of anger, depression etc., I may ask "What do you put in the search engine for that?" Other narrative style questions include "What advice do you give yourself to get you through tough times?" Metaphors can be helpful to re-envision future directions, such as, "What is a seed worth planting?" and "What skills have you been quietly tucking away, that can guide you on the next stage of your journey?"

Clients will share their history of painful events or shameful secrets when they have decided they feel safe with you. To begin with, the first session can be more of a casual chat, with the counsellor asking questions about support networks, how the person usually gets through hard times, what life hopes they have held onto through stormy weather, or what peak moments they have enjoyed or celebrated in their life.

We need to be slow and curious, not fast and furious. Until trust is established, we need to be comfortable with gradual, incremental client engagement.

> "For fast acting relief,
> try slowing down."
> — LILY TOMLIN

3. The Client

From the client's perspective, counselling is often a last resort when the problem has depleted their biopsychosocial resources. Perhaps shame has silenced them, or they have never verbalised the effects of past trauma, and now some incident has prompted then to reach out. Each one will be facing some adversity and possibly have lost a great deal of hope for recovery.

> "There is nothing in a caterpillar
> that tells you it's going to be a butterfly."
> — R. BUCKMINSTER FULLER

Some people arrive feeling weighed down by some existential question, or have thoughts about themself as having failed. They may be considering ending their life. It can help to ask, "Who else actually knows this is how you're feeling right now?"

Often nobody else knows. As a result, many people begin to live isolated lives. Hiding the truth can be a survival response: combining both the flight and freeze responses to painful events and memories.

Hope may have dwindled, and this can create quite an expectation that we, with our fancy qualifications, can somehow work miracles. Magic can happen in counselling with memorable turning points and aha moments, but it is also the result of hard work!

If we get a feeling the client may not be 'ready' to engage in therapy, we can ask, "How did you come to decide to have some counselling?" This open-ended question may reveal that it was their boss's or their friend's idea, and we may ask further about their readiness and willingness to do the hard work of therapy. We can ask, "Why is counselling important to you right now? What's at stake?" Maybe a partner has delivered an ultimatum.

We may be the only person in their life who is willing or capable of hearing and holding their pain.

4. The Ethics

The first meeting is a pivotal moment to explain privacy, consent and confidentiality. I say, "Confidentiality is always limited, and conditional around my belief whether another person, or yourself, may be unsafe, especially a child. If I was concerned about safety, I would speak with you first and ask you who you think might be a suitable person for me to speak with, to ensure risks to safety are reduced. Our profession has strict guidelines about responding to risk and safety, and I will be guided by my duty of care."

Clients need to understand our qualifications and registration status, and know where to look to understand how the profession is regulated, what their rights are, and if necessary, how to make a complaint.

After the consent papers are signed, I discuss how we will know if we are on track, and how to exchange feedback. "If either of us feels there's a misunderstanding, or a change is needed, it would be best if we can both name and discuss these things, which will arise from time to time'.

In this profession, our own self-care and the boundaries we set are intertwined. I have learnt the hard way that a clear explanation about session times, contact in between sessions, payment of fees and cancellations need to be central to the client intake discussion. During that intake phone call, I say, "The session will be 50 minutes from the appointment start time, and after 45 minutes we generally stop and allow those last five minutes for a debrief to see how the session went. How does that sound to you?"

When asked if I can work weekends, or make other exceptions, I have learnt a lifesaving two letter word:

> "No is a complete sentence."
> — SUSAN GREGG

When working with separating parents, we need to be clear about whether we write court reports or not, and routinely ask about and assess risk around client safety and the safety of the children from family violence, as well as a partner's suicide risk.

In couples or family work, I always ask for copies of AVOs and court orders, and I never speak to, or email a lawyer without taking legal advice.

Documenting each of these steps in our case notes is vital. The counsellor must remember that at any time, a court can subpoena their case files. Your registration body can assist with these matters.

It is important to know that one day you may be on the witness stand at the Coroner's Court, being asked "What did you ask the client on that last session about their thoughts of suicide? Where is the evidence of your risk assessment? What is your training in this area?"

Sometimes we may meet with a client who reveals they have a complex PTSD diagnosis, a serious mental health condition, psychosis, eating disorders, addictions or live with a chronic history of suicide attempts. Usually, our gut will tell us when a presentation is beyond our clinical competence. Our code of ethics directs us to make referrals to more qualified mental health practitioners when such serious difficulties arise.

Some agencies are great at providing excellent peer and group supervision and generally looking after their team's wellbeing. We cannot stay well in this field alone. Having a sense of belonging and connection with our peers is invaluable.

Burnout is a painful, complex human reaction to ongoing stress, and a sense that your inner resources have run dry. This becomes an ethical issue, as both the client and you will be negatively impacted.

> "The cure for burnout isn't, and can't be, self-care.
> It has to be all of us caring for each other."
> — EMILY AND AMELIA NAGOSKI

As counsellors, we may be fooling ourselves that we are juggling our life well enough. But what is your gut saying? Are you perhaps managing stress by falling into unhealthy ways to artificially unwind?

The "last client of the day," at the end of a busy week will probably not get the five-star unconditional positive regard, empathic version of yourself, and is that ok? I found some interesting research saying "The probability of the anaesthesiologist's mistake actually harming the patient was 0.3% at 8 a.m. and 1% at 3 p.m. The researchers attributed these errors to 'afternoon circadian lows,' which decrease physician vigilance." (https://www.thehealthy.com/healthcare/never-go-to-hospital-afternoon/)

What is your own body signal that lets you know it's time to pause, and recalibrate the work-play-rest balance? Put you hand on your belly and heart now, press slightly and exhale. Ask yourself, "How is my self-care going?" We need to reconnect with our body every day.

> "There are 1,440 minutes in a day,
> Make sure you spend a few looking after you."
> — UNKNOWN

Along the way, counsellors can hit the wall. Maybe they keep forgetting to use that two-letter word, "No." It can be delusional to keep donning that dazzling, superhero cape and believe we are invincible. It has happened to me.

I say to my supervisees who are accelerating towards burnout: "Nobody is likely to tap you on the shoulder and say, "Hi, can I offer you a nine-day fortnight, and a reduced caseload for a while?"

Only we ourselves can ask for what we need. The question I most often ask in supervision when such matters arise, is "Is this sustainable?" A deep exhale is usually followed by, "No!"

To avoid burnout, we can be clear and firm with our boundaries, create daily routines that support our wellbeing, and seek regular supervision with a person with whom we can be honest.

> "Doesn't matter if the glass is half-empty or half-full.
> All that matters is that you are the one pouring the water."
> — **MARK CUBAN**

Conclusion

Counselling is a demanding, sometimes stressful, inspiring, fulfilling and wonderful vocation.

To stay well, you need to put yourself at the top of your "to do" list, and regularly offer yourself warm and encouraging self-talk. Lean into regular, supportive supervision and creative reflective practices. You can't pour from an empty cup, so it is up to us to find what works for us: making time for music and art, joyful ventures, and a mix of solitude and down-times with low-impact friends and family.

> "There are no qualifications for the kind of person I must be. What is wanted... is a person who will be present."
> — EUGENE T. GENDLIN

We will always be a "work in progress."

Stay connected to yourself and may your journey be blessed.

Bio:

I am grateful to have been able to build a meaningful counselling career. I wrote my first book, *A Counsellor's Companion* as a way to pass forward my knowledge and understanding about ways to support children and families experiencing life challenges. My own clinical background includes co-facilitating Men's Behaviour Change Programs, crisis and general tele-counselling, child and family counselling, specialist family violence counselling, EAP brief therapy counselling, family bereavement counselling and individual and group clinical supervision. For over 30 years, I had also been delivering training.

My therapeutic practice includes liberal doses of mindfulness, narrative therapy, compassion-focused therapy (CFT), somatic focusing, acceptance and commitment therapy (ACT), creative and expressive playful therapy, existential therapy, life journey identity work, and befriending emotions using metaphors and storytelling.

Having said that, every new client invites me to create a unique, new approach, and my longevity in counselling has been assisted by a beginner's mind, creativity and a quirky authenticity.

Website: https://www.kimbillington.com.au

Qualifications:
B. Ed; M. Couns; M. Narrative Therapy & Community Work.

CHAPTER 12

"You Can Land Safely Here," said the Blank Page

By Kim Billington (ed)

When clients tell me they write, I explore this creative sparkle further: "How did you first come to write? How do words help? What relief do you find? Might you call this a form of self-therapy, or self-soothing? Is this something so spontaneous, that it doesn't even need editing?"

After trauma, from time to time, our inner world can rise up with such determination, we can feel compelled to express these unseen, unheard, and sometimes strong and scary emotions. Akin to the process of vomiting, once out, we can see our words saying what we had previously only felt. We may feel a lot better afterwards too. It may be less messy than cutting.

This chapter offers a walk-through the inner worlds of both my own journey, and those of others who have generously offered to share a poem that contributed to a therapeutic release.

May these tender and powerful expressions inspire you to pick up a pen when you next feel overwhelmed. This might also be a good fit for a client: "The blank page is a safe space. Maybe writing could help you to explore what your inner life wishes to say."

> "Give sorrow words.
> The grief that does not speak
> Knits up the o'er wrought heart
> and bids it break."
> — **WILLIAM SHAKESPEARE**

We may write to purge, to reach out in silent rage, sorrow or longing. Once written, we can let go. Poems can be cradles to soothe our soul. Poems can speak when our other voices run dry.

Here is a little story about how a woman I recently met created a poetic phrase to express her trauma, loss and fear.

I was up in the Dandenong Ranges of Victoria a month after winter storms had ravaged the small villages nestled among the luscious giant tree ferns and huge 80-metre gumtrees. Hundreds of trees had fallen, blocking access to everyone on the mountain and damaging power lines and property. It took 20 days to restore power!

For the previous 18 months, the community also had been hit hard by multiple pandemic lockdowns. Their tourism economy was already fragile, so their hopes and excitement when tourists could at last visit were cruelly dashed when the massive storm hit.

"YOU CAN LAND SAFELY HERE," SAID THE BLANK PAGE

The day I visited Sassafras was fiercely windy, with gusts up to 67km/h, and 570 trees had been uprooted overnight. I met Di Harbourd, owner of a handcraft shop who looked troubled. She mentioned that the wind was worrying her. I was her only customer and she spoke quietly about her experiences in the recent storm, and how the close community had all suffered terribly. The community's resilience was hanging by a thread. Di paused, and after a moment of reflection, said:

> "It's hard when the very thing you love
> is what hurts you."

We stood and nodded together at this sage reflection. She later wrote a letter to me, saying the local Facebook page had several pages of poetry after the storm, with school children also writing for healing. Di said, "Kids can be very profound and can write powerful pieces too." In my first book, 12-year-old Zoë wrote a poem about her life's extremes. Narrative therapy values the client's own words and phrases, which supports the use of poetry as a creative, expressive art.

Bessel van der Kolk also talked about the benefits of finding words and writing. He quotes J. W. Pennebaker's research showing writing increased self-understanding and even immune function.

A poem is wisdom on wings and connects us to ourselves and others. We hear the poem's song in our heart, and our whole being is moved. Poems can broaden our understanding of the whole human kit and caboodle. A poem can seize the bitterness of suffering, and sweeten it with the hope of being heard and seen.

Being Kind
By DJ Hose

Being kind to myself
I'm fighting for my survival
It's ok that I'm struggling
It's ok that I'm crying at the trivial

Being kind to myself
There are things I can't do right now
Focusing on what I can do at this moment
Focusing on how far I've come
Being kind to myself

EMANCIPATION
By Michelle Fairbrother

Growing toward a space skilfully forbidden for centuries
Furtively at first
Hesitantly treading unfamiliar ground
Longing for a place I have never been
For a self I have never known
The malignant truth buried under 'shoulds' and 'musts'
Clinging to who I wish I was
Despite the suffocating demands to be
The 'right' kind of woman,
The 'right' kind of worker, daughter, mother
Falling in line and knowing my place
Scales tumbling from my eyes
Behind rose-tinted glasses that would never fit

With terror beating in my chest
Choosing this dangerous unsteady ground
Over what is implicitly encouraged
The image of the other obedient woman

now existing only in painful memories
But not yet sure who is taking her place
Knowing who I refuse to be
Yet struggling with who I never was

Relief and gratitude flood over me like a hot flush
I am not alone, I never was
We are women, we are warriors
Ancient, wise and worthy

Rock Bottom Friday
By Kim Billington

I can pretend I am well to my friends no more,
Life has pounded me 'til I'm smashed like rocks on the shore.
I'm a jigsaw puzzle that's been knocked and shaken:
Into the despair of my life I now awaken.

I am numb, I am stunned, I am weak, I am still,
No more tears seem to flow, my soul is so ill.
I can't clean the house, I can't even call it home,
And how will I pay the dentist, the rego, the phone?

And what will happen next? Even Lifeline's done their bit,
There's no one else I'll burden, so I'll finish what I've writ.
At least I've kissed my children, and said, "Goodnight, sleep well."
Oh, sad it is on nights like this I live so close to hell.

Exhausted at last, and these words are all out,
Perhaps God will now show me what the fuss was about.

(Written late at night on 14/08/1998 when my youngest was 10 months old.)

Reality Bites
By Jenny Lo Ricco (Author of *Facing Your Pain*)

Find it hard to go to sleep
When the black dog bites my heels
Many thoughts go through my head
And restlessness I feel.

Reliving the experience
The hurt that grows inside.
Some days I see the positives.
Some days I want to hide.

Some days I'm dragging myself
Out of bed to face the day
The pain that's in my body
Can at times drive me insane.

Don't want to be reliant
On the feeding times of drugs
I want to be as healthy
As before my back got stuck.

This changed my world forever
And made me feel so slow.
It made life so much harder
Than before I had the blow.

But then I have these days between
Where my pain has slipped away
I can get out and enjoy myself
See the joy in my whole day.

These are the ones I treasure.
The times where joy can last.
It helps me to remember
That the down times
They do pass.

His Invisible Self
By Hellena Bazán *(Author of* Are You Ready for Your Awakening?*)*

I fell in love with a man,
with his imperfections,
with his insecurities,
with his resentment.

I fell in love with his passion, his desires, his scent, his smile, his eyes,
his wisdom, his pain, his joy.

I fell in love with his invisible self, so sudden, so quick, so strong.

I shone my light as bright as I could
to keep him out of the dark,
to help him see the beauty I saw in him.

I fell in love with a man who didn't know what to do with such love.
He saw it's beauty,
He saw the promise,
and yet,
He chose to travel alone,
back into darkness.

I am the LIGHT,
I am the LOVE,
I am the TRUTH.

I walk beside him, always will,
but this time the radiance is mine.

A Counselling Secret
By Kim Billington

Two people meet in a room.
How did that happen?
The Cosmos sent this person for our mutual lessons.
There's a façade that 'we' are here to 'help' the other.
But we are all here to learn and grow.
In moments of countertransference,
Your lesson is revealed.

Examples of exploring the writing process
Q: How does writing a poem make a difference?

It creates an outlet. It provides me with a safe platform that can move that excess energy out, and remove the weight of what I am feeling.

Q: Did the poem write itself, in a flow, or was this finished poem the result of multiple drafts?

One draft. Usually they write themselves, especially if I am writing for therapeutic reasons.

About the Illustrator

Chris Munro is a Sydney-born artist who has previously worked for Walt Disney Television Animation and ABC Kids TV. He lives in Melbourne with a very bossy cat named Rocco.

Email: fishscaleshingle@yahoo.com

References by Chapter

Acknowledgement

ABC. *Gambay: a map of Australia's first languages.* https://www.abc.net.au/indigenous/features/gambay-languages-map/

AIATSIS. *Map of Indigenous Australia.* https://www.aiatsis.gov.au/explore/map-indigenous-australia

Koskela. *18 books on Australian Indigenous languages that will move and shake you.* https://www.koskela.com.au/blogs/news/25-books-on-indigenous-history-and-culture

History Victoria. *Australian Aboriginal History – Podcast Series.* https://www.historyvictoria.org.au/resources/australian-aboriginal-history-podcast-series/

Victorian Aboriginal Heritage Council. *Bunurong Land Council Aboriginal Corporation.* https://www.aboriginalheritagecouncil.vic.gov.au/bunurong-land-council-aboriginal-corporation

Opening quote

Eugene T. Gendlin; University of Chicago, U.S.A: http://www.previous.focusing.org/gendlin/docs/gol_2110.html

Chapter 1: Wuru Walking in Two Worlds with Annette Dudley

Dulwich Centre. *'Unspoken words.'* https://dulwichcentre.com.au/unspoken-words-creative-letters-to-elders-of-my-past-and-present-by-annette-dudley/

Metaphorically Speaking. *"Unearthing unspoken words"* with Annette Dudley. https://www.metaphoricallyspeaking.com.au/unspoken-words-annette-dudley/

Chapter 2: The Greatest Thing You'll Ever Learn… with Jackie Tarabay

Doka, K. J., & Martin, T. L. (2010). *Grieving beyond gender: Understanding the ways men and women mourn.* (2nd edition). Routledge.

Frankl, V. E. (2006). *Man's search for meaning: An introduction to logotherapy.* Beacon Press. (Original work published 1946).

Neimeyer, R. A. (2015). *Techniques of grief therapy: Creative practices for counselling the bereaved.* Routledge.

Thompson, B. E., & Neimeyer, R. A. (Eds.). (2014). *Grief and the expressive arts: Practices for creating meaning.* Routledge.

Worden, W. (2010). *Grief counselling and grief therapy: A handbook for the mental health practitioner.* Routledge.

Yalom, I. D. (1980). *Existential psychotherapy.* Basic Books.

Yalom, I. D. (2009a). *Staring at the sun: Overcoming the terror of death.* Jossey-Bass.

Yalom, I. D. (2009b). *The gift of therapy.* HarperCollins.

Yalom, I. D. (2013). *Love's executioner and other tales of psychotherapy.* Penguin Books.

For clients:

Cameron, J. (2016). *The artist's way: 25th anniversary edition.* Penguin Books.

Lesser, E. (2005). *Broken open: How difficult times can help us grow.* Villard.

Livingston, G. (2004). *Too soon old, too late smart: Thirty true things you need to know now.* Marlowe & Co.

Livingston, G. (2006). *Only spring: On mourning the death of my son.* Hachette Australia.

Livingston, G. (2009). *How to love: Choosing well at every stage of life.* Da Capo Life Long Books.

Livingston, G. (2012). *The thing you think you cannot do: Thirty truths about fear and courage.* Hachette Australia.

Rinpoche, S. (1992). *The Tibetan book of living and dying.* HarperCollins.

Sandberg, S. (2017). *Option B: Facing adversity, building resilience, and finding joy.* W H Allen.

Links:
Making Sense of Trauma. *Flashback Protocol.* https://www.makingsenseoftrauma.com/wp-content/uploads/2016/04/Flashback-Protocol.pdf

Chapter 3: Family Violence Through the Lens of Trauma with Dajana Sprajcer-Simeunovic

Bush, A. D. (2015). *Simple self-care for therapists: Restorative practices to weave through your workday.* W.W. Norton & Company.

Fisher, J. (2021). *Transforming the living legacy of trauma: A workbook for survivors and therapists.* Pesi Publishing & Media.

Rothschild, B. (2010). *The body remembers: The psychophysiology of trauma and trauma treatment.* New York: Norton.

van der Kolk, B. A. (2015). *The body keeps the score: Brain, mind and body in the healing of trauma.* Penguin.

Links:
1800 Respect. National sexual assault, domestic family violence counselling service. https://www.1800respect.org.au

Autplay Therapy. https://www.autplaytherapy.com/about-autplay-therapy/resources/

Domestic Violence Resource Centre Victoria. https://dvrcv.org.au

The Lookout. *For family violence workers.* https://www.thelookout.org.au/family-violence-workers

Insight Timer. [App]. https://insighttimer.com

Chapter 4: Outside My Comfort Zone with Susan Konstantas

Harris, R., & Hayes, S. C. (2009). *ACT made simple: An easy-to-read primer on acceptance and commitment therapy.* Oakland, California: New Harbinger Publications.

Hone, L. (2017). *Resilient grieving: How to find your way through devastating loss: A practical guide to recovery.* A & U New Zealand.

Mcgoldrick, M., Gerson, R., & Petry, S. S. (2008). *Genograms: Assessment and intervention.* W.W. Norton & Co.

Rhodes, P., & Wallis, A. (2011). *A practical guide to family therapy: Structured guidelines and key skills.* Ip Communications.

Williams, A. (2021). *Sink or swim.* Ultimate World Publishing.

Chapter 5: Finding the Rainbow Connection with Pamela Cox

Chaplin, J. (1999). *Feminist counselling in action.* Sage.

Egan, G., & Reese, R. J. (2019). *The skilled helper: A problem-management and opportunity-development approach to helping* (11th ed.). Cengage.

Links:

CASA agencies are community based, not-for-profit sexual assault counselling services including a 24-hour Sexual Assault Crisis Line (SACL).

https://gaymenshealth.com.au/

REFERENCES BY CHAPTER

Chapter 6: Evolution Not Revolution: The Challenge of Simple, Hard Work with Tom Lothian

De Becker, G. (1998). *The gift of fear: Survival signals that protect us from violence.* Dell.

Doidge, N. (2007) *The brain that changes itself: Stories of personal triumph from the frontiers of brain science.* New York: Viking.

Gladwell, M. (2006). *Blink: The power of thinking without thinking.* Penguin.

Yalom, I. D. (2013). *Love's executioner and other tales of psychotherapy.* Penguin Books.

App: Smiling Mind – https://www.smilingmind.com.au

Chapter 7: It's Never Too Late… For Secure Relationships to Blossom and Grow with Robyn Ball

Brownlee, P. (2007). *Magic places: The adult's guide to young children's creative art work.* New Zealand Playcentre Federation.

Brownlee, P. (2008). *Dance with me in the heart: The adult's guide to great infant-parent partnerships.* New Zealand Playcentre Federation.

Grille, R. (2009). *Parenting for a peaceful world.* Longueville Media.

Hoffman, K. et al. (2017) *Raising a secure child: How circle of security parenting can help you nurture your child's attachment, emotional resilience, and freedom to explore.* The Guilford Press.

Saltzberg, B. (2010). *Beautiful oops!* Workman Publishing Company.

Links:

Center on the Developing Child, Harvard University. https://www.developingchild.harvard.edu

Circle of Security International. https://www.circleofsecurityinternational.com/

Circle of Security International. (2015, Nov 10). *Being-With and Shark Music.* [Video]. Vimeo. https://vimeo.com/145329119

Mindaroo Foundation. https://www.thrivebyfive.org.au/

UMass Boston. (2009, Nov 30). *Still Face Experiment: Dr. Edward Tronick.* [Video]. Youtube. https://www.youtube.com/watch?v=apzXGEbZht0

Imbo, Frederick. (2020, Mar 4). *How not to take things personally?* [Video]. Youtube. https://www.youtube.com/watch?v=LnJwH_PZXnM

Robyn Gobbel. *Free resources.* https://www.robyngobbel.com/freeresources/

Chapter 8: Releasing Hidden Creativity as an Aid to Therapy with Dalit Bar

Lett, W. (1992). *How the arts make a difference in therapy.* South Melbourne, Australia. Australian Dance Council, (Victoria).

Malchiodi, C. (2012). *Handbook of art therapy.* NY, London. The Guilford Press.

McNiff, S. (2004). *Art heals: How creativity cures the soul.* Shambhala.

Chapter 9: More Than Just a Counsellor with Nothara Suraweera

Calm. [App]. https://www.calm.com.

Mental Health Academy. https://www.mentalhealthacademy.com.au/

QLife. https://www.qlife.org.au/

Reach Out. https://au.reachout.com/

Chapter 10: Hearing the Voice of the Child with Kim Billington

Brach, T. (2020). *Radical compassion: Learning to love yourself and your world with the practice of RAIN.* Rider Books.

Madsen, W. C. (2011). Collaborative Helping Maps: A tool to guide thinking and action in family-centered services. *In Family Process* 50.4: 529– 543, 2011.

Neff , K. (2015). *Self compassion: Stop beating yourself up and leave insecurity behind.* Yellow Kite.

Siegel, D. J. & Hartzell, M. (2004). *Parenting from the inside out.* New York: Penguin.

Stahl, S., & Lauffer, E. (2020). *The child in you: The breakthrough method for bringing out your authentic self.* Penguin Books.

Wolynn, M. (2017). *It didn't start with you: How inherited family trauma shapes who we are and how to end the cycle.* Penguin Books.

Links:

Maté, Dr. G. (2020, Dec 27). *How to BECOME a BETTER PARENT: Positive vs Toxic Parenting Tips.* [Video]. Youtube. https://youtu.be/fcPPDbvGr7s

Play Therapy Institute of Colorado. *Lisa Dion Discusses the Myth that "Regulation" Means Calm.* [Video]. Youtube. https:// www.youtube.com/watch?v=4cwW2IIP6AA

Psychotherapy Networker. (2017) *How to locate your "felt sense."* https://www.psychotherapynetworker.org/blog/details/1267/how-to-locate-your-felt-sense

Tuning Into Kids. (2020, May 21). *Emotion Coaching DVD.* [Video]. Youtube. https://youtu.be/jWJlRTi7YH8

Brown, Dr. S. (2008, May). [Video]. TED. https://www.ted.com/talks/stuart_brown_play_is_more_than_just_fun

Positive Discipline. *Family Meetings.* https://www.positivediscipline.com/articles/family-meetings

Kim's YouTube links:

Conversations with parents about what they admire about their child: https://youtu.be/g3WvWe_t9QM

Meeting our anger with mindfulness: https://youtu.be/gmvG88_nnPM

Our younger self: using the babushka doll: https://youtu.be/6rC4rH3CcKE

Parents: improving the connection with your child: https://youtu.be/zCY8nvKu57w

Working with parents: https://youtu.be/Kq7K6z8OyQI

Chapter 11: Four Cornerstones of Counselling

Qualification references:

Australian Counselling Association. https://www.aca@theaca.net.au

Australian Institute of Professional Counsellors. https://www.aipc.net.au

Australian Psychologial Society. https://www.psychology.org.au/

Deakin University. *What's the difference between psychology and counselling?* https://www.deakin.edu.au/articles/study-areas/psychology/whats-the-difference-between-psychology-and-counselling

Good Therapy. *Types of therapists.* https://www.goodtherapy.com.au/flex/types-of-therapists/906/1

Psychotherapy and Counselling Federation of Australia. https://www.pacfa.org.au/

Tafe Courses. https://www.tafecourses.com.au/

References:

Cozolino, L. (2002). *The neuroscience of psychotherapy: Building and rebuilding the human brain.* New York: Norton.

Dana, D., & Porges, S. W. (2020). *Polyvagal exercises for safety and connection: 50 client-centered practices.* W.W. Norton & Company.

Doidge, N. (2007). *The Brain that changes itself: Stories of personal triumph from the frontiers of brain science.* New York: Viking, 2007.

Fisher, J. (2017). *Healing the fragmented selves of trauma survivors: Overcoming internal self-alienation.* Routledge, New York.

Hubble, M. A., Duncan, B. L., & Miller, S. D. (1999). *The heart and soul of change: What works in therapy.* Washington DC: American Psychological Association.

Johnson, S. M. (2018). *Attachment theory in practice: Emotionally focused therapy (EFT) with individuals, couples, and families.* New York: The Guilford Press.

Levine, P. A. (2008). *Healing trauma.* Boulder, CO: Sounds True.

Levine, P. (2010). *In an unspoken voice.* Berkeley: North Atlantic Books.

Ogden, P., Minton. K. & Pain, C. (2006). *Trauma and the body: A sensorimotor approach to psychotherapy.* New York: Norton.

REFERENCES BY CHAPTER

Porges, S. & Dana, D. (2018). *Clinical applications of the Polyvagal Theory: The emergence of polyvagal-Informed therapies.* New York: Norton.

Rothschild, B. (2010). *The body remembers: The psychophysiology of trauma and trauma treatment.* New York: Norton.

Rothschild, B. (2011). *Trauma essentials: The go-to guide.* New York: Norton.

Siegel, Daniel J. (2009). *Mindsight.* New York: Random House.

van der Kolk, B. A. (2015). *The body keeps the score: Brain, mind and body in the healing of trauma.* Penguin.

Wallin, D. J. (2007). *Attachment in psychotherapy.* New York: The Guilford Press.

Links:

Australian Bureau of Statistics. (2016). *Personal Safety, Australia.* https://www.abs.gov.au/statistics/people/crime-and-justice/personal-safety-australia/latest-release

Escalante, A. (2020, Aug 11) *Researchers doubt that certain mental disorders are disorders at all.* https://www.forbes.com/sites/alisonescalante/2020/08/11/researchers-doubt-that-certain-mental-disorders-are-disorders-at-all/?sh=6e1e527815a6

Dulwich Centre. *Collaborative helping maps: a simple map to transform relational positioning.* https://dulwichcentre.com.au/collaborative-helping-maps-a-simple-map-to-transform-relational-positioning-by-bill-madsen

Powell, A and Harris, L. *'See What You Made Me Do' is must-watch TV. Here's what needs to happen now to address domestic abuse.* https://www.sbs.com.au/news/see-what-you-made-me-do-is-must-watch-tv-here-s-what-needs-to-happen-now-to-address-domestic-abuse/0f1b8629-90d8-4a8c-a5c1-f4dec59994f9

Twenty new conversations around suicide. *Counselling Australia Journal* 21.3 (2020): 26. https://www.theaca.net.au/journals/ACAMagVol21No3.pdf

Henri Nowen Society. (2021) *Listening as spiritual hospitality.* https://www.henrinouwen.org/meditation/listening-spiritual-hospitality/

Hess, Nicole. *A neuroscientific perspective on the therapeutic alliance and how talking changes the brain: Supporting a common factors model of psychotherapy.* https://www.pacja.org.au/2019/12/a-neuroscientific-perspective-on-the-therapeutic-alliance-and-how-talking-changes-the-brain-supporting-a-common-factors-model-of-psychotherapy-2/

Koncz A, Demetrovics Z and Takacs Z. "Meditation interventions efficiently reduce cortisol levels of at-risk samples: a meta-analysis." *Health Psychology Review* 15.1 (2021): 56-84. https://www.tandfonline.com/doi/full/10.1080/17437199.2020.1760727

Maté, Dr. G. (2019, May 15). Gabor Maté – *Authenticity vs Attachment*. [Video]. Youtube. https://youtu.be/l3bynimi8HQ

Miriam Rose Foundation. (2017, Nov 8). *DADIRRI*. [Video]. Youtube. https://youtu.be/tow2tR_ezL8

NICABM. (2017, Jun 3). Treating Trauma: 2 Ways to Help Clients Feel Safe, with Peter Levine. [Video]. Youtube. https://www.youtube.com/watch?v=G7zAseaIyFA

NICABM. (2015, Nov 15). *How to use the Wisdom of the body to heal PTSD and trauma – with Pat Ogden, PhD*. [Video]. Youtube. https://youtu.be/sw3iTW_Nqw4

Turp, Elizabeth. (2017, Jul 1). *10 self-care lessons you can learn from a counsellor*. https://www.thecounsellorscafe.co.uk/single-post/2017/06/26/10-self-care-lessons-you-can-learn-from-a-Counsellor

Victoria State Government. (2020, May 19). *Mandatory Reporting – DHHS Service Providers*. https://providers.dffh.vic.gov.au/mandatory-reporting

Chapter 12: "You Can Land Safely Here," said the Blank Page by Kim Billington (ed)

Bolton, G., Field, V., & Thompson, K. (2006). *Writing works: A resource handbook for therapeutic writing workshops and activities*. London: Jessica Kingsley Publishers.

Fox, J. (1995). *Finding what you didn't lose*. New York, NY: J.P. Tarcher.

Links:

Raab, Diana. (2021, Apr 7). *The Power of Poetry Therapy*. https://www.psychologytoday.com/us/blog/the-empowerment-diary/202104/the-power-poetry-therapy

Poetry Therapy. https://www.poetrytherapy.org/

Offers

Purchasing this book is just the beginning. You can now access any of these three offers. Contact Kim via her website Counselling Conversations: www.kimbillington.com.au.

1. SUPERVISION: For those who require monthly supervision of their clinical practice (through ACA and PACFA etc.), Kim is offering a one-off 30% discount for a supervision session on purchase of this book.

2. SPEAKER: Engage Kim to speak at your event. Kim can be booked to be a guest speaker at your university, workplace, radio station, school, parenting group or community hub through the enquiries page on her website. Refer to the speaker bio page for Kim's range of parenting topics. After purchasing any five copies of Kim's books, Kim will create a free, 60-minute online guest speaker/webinar tailored to your needs.

3. RESOURCES: Kim has free, printable PDFs of valuable resources via her website.

Kim Billington

With over 30 years' work with families, Kim Billington is an expert in the field of counselling, parenting, family issues and facilitation of group activities. She is a dynamic and engaging speaker who brings fun and experiential activities to her speaking. Her audiences walk away with practical skills they can take home to their families.

Kim has two Masters' degrees in Counselling and Narrative Therapy, and a Bachelor of Education. She originally worked in local government agencies such as the City of Melbourne and the City of Port Phillip as a specialist parent support worker. Kim became a counselling supervisor and successfully transitioned her business online in 2020 during the global pandemic and is continuing to support families and fellow counsellors in learning what works for them.

Kim is an acclaimed author of two books – the Number 1 Amazon Best Seller, A Counsellor's Companion and the recently released Counselling Conversations. Her passion is to hear the voice of the child and believes that children are the centre of the world.

Kim is a highly sought-after speaker who leaves her audiences fully empowered. Kim can create a custom presentation to suit your specific audience and time considerations, however her signature talks include:

Create Your Unique Family Roadmap
- How to move from Chaos to Connection
- How to change Tears to Triumph
- Unlock what really matters to you

Family Pitstop – Noticing Rattles in the Engine?
- How does your family make sense of anger?
- What soft whispers might you be missing in your family?
- How to create a safe place where everyone is heard

What's really under the hood?
- Unpack Your Epic Failures
- Rear view mirror reflections from your own past
- Discovering moments of Harmony

To enquire about booking Kim as a speaker at your next event, email:
counsellingconversations@gmail.com
or go to: www.kimbillington.com.au
for pricing and availabilities.

Reflections

REFLECTIONS

www.ingramcontent.com/pod-product-compliance
Lightning Source LLC
Chambersburg PA
CBHW071609080526
44588CB00010B/1070